End Of Days
9/11 and the War on Faith

ISBN
978-0-6152-4504-1

To Maytal. Thanks for being my friend.

"…When the Son of man cometh, shall he find
faith on the earth?"
-Luke 18:8

Contents

Forward

Almost exactly a year ago, I set out to answer the question that has been at the forefront of American politics for most of this short century; what I think of the Iraq war. I thought it would be an easy question to answer, but it proved to be a larger project than I ever imagined.

It took me through places in history I never dreamed of, and I have read books I never wanted to read; *Mein Kampf, The Communist Manifesto, Utopia.* Altogether, I read some fifty books doing research for the small tome I present to you.

Why so much hard work to express an opinion? Because what I found was that 9/11 and the invasion of Iraq are part of a bigger story, one that goes back for centuries. Indeed, 9/11 is a part of the ongoing struggle between good and evil, but when the evidence is examined, it becomes increasingly clear that we have become confused about who the good guys and the bad guys are.

This book chronicles the real war we are involved in, of which 9/11 is only a chapter. That larger war is a worldwide phenomenon, and it is far more insidious than I ever imagined when I began this journey.

This story is the story of our time, and our place in it. I am laying out, for the first time that I am aware of, not just the facts of 9/11, but the story behind the events. I have written this as a primer for Christians, Muslims, and Jews as well as anyone who still cares about the traditional values that helped build our civilizations.

The bad news is we have been snookered. We have been played by our enemies for their own gain. The good news is that there is a way out of the abyss if we can gather the political and economic will to take it. It is my heartfelt prayer that we find a way to do so before it is too late.

Thomas Spriggs,
July 13, 2008

Introduction

If I live until July of 2030, I will be 67 years old.

I will also be held in a prison camp, surrounded by razor wire and heavily guarded as I wait to be "reintegrated" into society. There will be dozens of these camps spread all across America in out of the way places so that the good people of the nation do not have to see what goes on in them.

For expediency, they will be set up in abandoned factories and warehouses in the countryside and near small towns. Abandoned military bases and other sites of that type will be pressed into service. There will be hundreds of these camps across America.

Food, water, and shelter from the weather will not be provided. Outside the razor wire, heavy equipment will dig large trenches to hold the bodies of those who have been "processed". The people who enter the buildings to be "processed" will leave them as corpses. Most will simply starve or die from the exposure before getting that far.

Most likely, my family I and will have been dragged from our home in the middle of the night. Our books, computers, cell phones, and even our personal effects will be gathered up and taken to the local Homeland Security to be pored over. They will tear through everything we own, looking for evidence.

Evidence that we are believers.

I will be joined by any Muslims and Jews who are unfortunate enough to live in the region. We will be separated from our families, sleeping in the mud or dirt, eating what few scraps we are afforded by our captors, without the basic necessities of life, as we wait our turn to die.

All Churches, Mosques, and Synagogues will be confiscated by Homeland Security. Many of the older buildings will be razed in the night, as our spiritual leaders and their families are executed without as much as a trial. It will make Hitler's Night of Broken Glass look like play pretend.

All across Europe and America untold millions will die for no other reason than the fact that they believe in a monotheistic God who provides his highest creation moral guidelines. The Bible, Torah, and Qu'ran will be outlawed, and all copies of them destroyed. Nonbelievers will be forced to turn in any copies they may possess, and possession of these texts will be grounds for immediate termination.

As bad as it will be in America, Europe will be even bloodier. Events in America will send a signal to the Europeans that they may deal with the Muslims who have intruded on their lands with a free reign. Every nation in Europe will mobilize its military and police forces to strike against the Muslim community.

It will begin where it left off, in Kosovo. The international peacekeeping force there will quietly slip away, leaving the Albanian Muslims and their allies in the region exposed once again to the brutal policy of "ethnic cleansing".

And the Serbs, like the rest of Europe, will not be taking prisoners. Muslims will simply be killed wherever they are found, period. The roads to Albania will once again be choked with refugees fleeing the slaughter. Only this time, there will be no safe place to hide. Serbian troops will quickly overwhelm the unprepared Albanian military and conquer the country in weeks.

The rest of Europe will be just as bloody. The nations of NATO will waste no time crushing Muslim neighborhoods and brutally murdering all Muslim inhabitants, including women and children. It will be one of the greatest slaughters of history, perpetrated by people who pride themselves on their civilized way of life.

The few Muslims who manage to escape the original onslaught will find they have nowhere to hide. Interpol will become the new Gestapo, rounding up all the Christians, Jews, and Muslims they can find. People of faith will be hunted like animals.

India will do likewise, and a civil war will break out between Indian troops and the people in the Muslim part of the Kashmir region. Just like in Europe, they will not stop until they have rid themselves of Muslims altogether. Thousands of Muslims will flee to Pakistan to seek refuge. But to their dismay, they will find that no place on earth is secure.

The nations of the West will have no intentions of stopping; their ultimate triumph will be within their grasp. Once they "secure" themselves from within, they will move to end the existence of their enemies once and for all. Every nation in the Middle East, Including Israel, will be given an ultimatum; surrender or die. But death is coming to them either way.

Of course Israel and Islam will not comply. They will fight to the death to defend themselves and their people. The ultimate showdown in the history of mankind is about to commence. And it will be worse than the most horrible nightmare ever conjured.

Cairo, Jerusalem, Tehran, and Damascus will be destroyed in the middle of the night by a sneak nuclear attack, while India takes out the capital of Pakistan, Islamabad. This will be followed by one of the largest invasions in history, as 1.5 million men land on the shores of Israel and Lebanon and millions pour across the Indian border into Iran.

The huge NATO naval force in the Mediterranean will unleash an unprecedented amount of fire into the areas surrounding their beach heads. Entire villages will be wiped out, both Jewish and Lebanese. Once ashore, the Western armies will not be contained; armored units will strike deep into the surrounding countryside, crippling the ability of resisters to respond adequately.

By the end of the first week, Western armies will nearing the remains of Damascus and will have occupied two-thirds of Israel. Behind them, large groups of Homeland Security and Interpol agents will be busy rounding up and eliminating any remaining inhabitants. In many cases western infantry units will simply line up all of the survivors in a village and gun them down on the spot.

Islam, Judaism, and Christianity will be driven far underground. Any remaining believers will be tortured and killed if caught. To the public, this will look like a necessary step to ensure the future of all mankind. They will have been brainwashed by a media relentless in its criticism of faith and the dangers of religion.

Over time, the remaining pockets of belief will slowly be eradicated. No one can hide forever, and Western governments will be relentless in their pursuit of peoples of faith.

Within a few decades, there will be nothing left of the Abrahamic religions beyond a few pages in college textbooks and in electronic encyclopedias. Faith will be dead.

Impossible, you say? What if I could show you that the way is being prepared even as we speak, that the forces of darkness are gathering right now, and that they expect to begin seeing the fruit of their labors very soon?

That is what I intend this book to be-a roadmap to the destiny of our three great religions. We can stop them, but we must do so soon. Doing so will require that we lay aside our differences and prepare to change the way we deal with each other.

But before we can look forward, we must look back. We need to understand the roots of the war against faith and how it has changed over the roughly century and a half of conflict to understand who and what and where our enemy is.

We need to listen to the words of our opponents and take them seriously. We have always underestimated them, because we believe that God is on our side. But this is not magic, and we are not bulletproof. "Do your best, prepare for the worst—**then** trust God to bring victory," is the message of Proverbs 21:31.

Omar Bartov wrote a book review for the Jewish World Review on Hitler's second book, which was not published during his lifetime. In that review he gives us one of the most important statements of our times:

"...Hitler taught us more definitively than anyone else in history: some people, some regimes, some ideologies, some political programs, and, yes, some religious groups, must be taken at their word. Some people mean what they say, and say what they will do, and do what they said..."

"There are those who practice what they preach and are proud of it. They view those who act otherwise, who compromise and pull back from ultimate conclusions, as opportunists, as weaklings, as targets to be easily conquered and subdued by their own greater determination, hardness, and ruthlessness. When they say they will kill you, they will kill you--if you do not kill them first."

That is the nature of the struggle we face, and we cannot ignore it any longer. The enemy sees this as a fight to the death. *And they believe they are winning.* If we are to survive, we must defend ourselves now, while there is still time.

This book is written to many people. It is written to my fellow Americans who are living under a government by which we are not being told the truth and which we are no longer effectively controlling.

It is written to conservatives to expose the insanity that has penetrated the thinking of the conservative movement concerning our nation's international policies. We have truly become mindless sheeple, and it is time for us to wake from our slumber.

But most importantly, this book is meant as a primer to my brothers and sisters of the Abrahamic faiths. By the time you finish this work, I want you to fully understand the nature of the enemy we face and how we must respond if we are to survive.

This book is also written to our enemies. I have been exposing you systematically through my blogs on blogger.com and other web sites. I am now putting you on notice that you will no longer be able to manipulate and twist public opinion to your own sick philosophy. I may be the only person in the whole world willing to stand up and tell the truth about the nature of your crimes, but I will speak out regardless.

This is not a book for the faint of heart. You will find I am a meticulous researcher and back most of my claims with references. I encourage you to check all of my sources, and I encourage every American and European who is not Muslim to read *At the Heart of Terror* by Monte Palmer and Princess Palmer. I also recommend *The Enemy at Home* by Dinesh D'Souza for everyone. Americans have practically no clue as to what is happening in the Middle East, and these books will help rectify that fault.

But this work is more than an academic exercise; it is also a message grounded in the reality of our times. For as Mr. Bartov so eloquently points out, "Some people mean what they say, and say what they will do, and do what they said."

And to *that*, people of faith must respond- or die.

Chapter One
The Great Silence

"Three are even better, for a triple-braided cord is not
easily broken."
-Ecclesiastes 4:12b, New Living Translation

We will begin our study in the most
unlikely of places; the Holy Bible. While I am
aware that many people will not be interested in
this subject, I beg you to bear with me.
Superstition and hype have overwhelmed any
hopes of reasonable discourse on this subject, and
premilleniumism has become all the rage among
core believers of all three Abrahamic religions
(Christianity, Judaism, and Islam).

If we are ever to begin to bring some
sensibility to this subject, we must strip away the
innuendo and hyperbole and see the prophecies
as they are written, not as we wish to interpret
them. It may be human nature to use prophecy as
a tool to establish the superiority of our own

beliefs, but that is not an adequate answer to the coming destruction of our faiths. We need more than that.

I focus on the Bible because I am familiar with it, and have studied it for decades. I know where to look to find scriptural prophecy and the basics of what they mean. I do not claim to be a Biblical scholar, only that I know enough to point out a few basic facts concerning these passages. For this brief study, I will use the Living Bible and the King James.

We will only be looking at a few basic passages of scripture for this study. I wish to focus briefly on Ezekiel chapters 38 and 39, Isaiah 41, Daniel chapters 7, 11, and 12, along with Revelation chapters 13 and 16 through 19. I am not interested in the titillating details of battle, only the description of the government and culture that the Bible provides for the end days.

I am also not focusing solely on the role of the Jews as the target of the final world government's wrath, because I believe the description of the end times in the Bible gives tantalizing clues as to how the end-time process comes about, and that process involves the destruction of Christianity and Islam as well. Further, nowhere in the picture painted by the scriptures of Revelation does America directly appear, and I think I know why.

Prophetically speaking, Ezekiel chapters 38 and 39 seem to describe a separate battle from the others. And in the King James Version Libya, Persia, and Ethiopia are specifically mentioned as participants with the main antagonist, Gog. 38:8 calls it the "latter years", and the New Living Translation calls it "A long time from now" without further explanation. Many consider this the "trip wire" that begins the process leading to the Final Battle.

But this is the only place in these prophesies that mention the nations of the Middle East participating individually other than Israel. However, the other scriptures mention a different political division of the region that apparently occurs afterwards. But for a moment, let's take a look at what I believe are the only scriptures that refer to America. They are found in Isaiah chapter 41. I want to look at them in the New Living.

The first few verses describe the "lands beyond the sea" in fear of a conqueror who "meets victory at every step" (vs. 2). And verse 25 says, "I have stirred up a leader from the north and east" who will have victory over kings and princes.

Keep in mind that this is north and east of where Israel lies, and almost assuredly points to China. It is horribly unlikely to be America, because the "lands beyond the sea" fear this leader. Not only that, but the reason for their conquering is given as idolatry. But these are not idols of wood and stone, they are a different kind of idol.

There is a strange message to Israel beginning in verse 8 and spelled out in verse 10; "Don't be afraid, for I am with you. Do not be dismayed, for I am your God." Apparently, the events described in the previous verses are disturbing to the Jewish people.

The conclusion is simple; North America is eventually conquered by a brilliant Chinese General who seems unstoppable. Furthermore, verses 26 through 28 make it clear that God is placing his reputation on the line over this prophecy. "Who but I told you this would happen? Who else predicted this, making you admit he was right? *No one else said a word!*" (Italics mine).

Don't bother trying to find evidence supporting the validity of this prophecy elsewhere. American Christianity is too egocentric to admit the possibility of defeat. And like much of Islam, it has mingled religion and nationalism into a potent witches' brew of religious patriotism. To a certain extent, the American Churches believe America was founded not just on but *because* of Christian principles.

This means that for millions of American Christians, democracy is as much a part of their "religion" as communion or Sunday school is. They have blurred the line between faith and patriotism until it no longer exists. It is much like beating a square peg in a round hole, only in this case they beat on it until they *make* it fit.

I am not disparaging democracy in itself, and I believe that most people would agree with me about that, including Muslims. But democracy is a form of government and not a religious principle. There is a difference. But American Christians cannot see the difference and thus cannot admit to the validity of this chapter in Isaiah.

But what about Islam? What does the Bible tell us about the faith of Islam in the last days? This is a subject about which the Bible is strangely silent. Fortunately, there are clues in the text that point us towards why. So really quickly, let's look at the big picture of the prophecies involved.

It appears that Daniel chapter 7 and Revelation chapter 13 both describe the rise of a world power that is the very incarnation of evil. Note that they both have ten horns, but that three of the horns are replaced by one that blasphemes the name of God. These verses form the linchpin for Biblical prophecy. They also tell us something about our fate, both as Christians and Muslims.

Still using the New Living, let's review some of those verses in Daniel 7. Verse 23 tells us this beast will "devour the whole world, trampling everything in its path." The picture provided in the King James is that of the nations of the world being broken up. But it is in verse 25 that we have the clearest statement; "He will defy the Most High and wear down the holy people of the Most High."

This leader is warring against the people of faith he rules, or what is left of them. But it gets more interesting in the 11th and 12th chapters of Daniel. Here, we are given a closer look at the political wrangling that will lead to the Final Battle.

The first two leaders mentioned here are the king of the north and the king of the south. On the surface, he is talking about ancient kingdoms, but the first four verses of chapter twelve shows this prophecy is for the end times. To accentuate the point, Daniel is told flat-out in verse 9, "…what I have said is for the time of the end."

What we are left with is a regional conflict between two of the kingdoms of the Beast. The battle shifts back and forth without either side getting the upper hand. Then, a third man enters the arena. Verses 21 through 23 tell us he takes over by intrigue then conquers one of the other regions, forming an alliance with the third after that. Verse 24 tells us that this person will put in place a socialist economic system and will "distribute among his followers the plunder and wealth of the rich."

Verses 25 through 27 tell us that he will turn against the king of the south, but will be roundly defeated. However the king of the south will lack the forces necessary to finish off his new enemy. In verse 28, the king of the north withdraws and increases the persecution of people of faith.

Verses 29 through 39 tell us this ruler will attempt another invasion against the king of the south, but naval support will cause him to withdraw. Returning home again, he will now turn his attention to the Abrahamic believers in his kingdom, defiling their beliefs and turning them away from the faith.

Verses 40 through 45 tell us this king will be attacked by his neighbors to the north and to the south, but this time he defeats them roundly. He pushes back the king to the north then turns his fury on the king of the south, conquering all of northwest Africa all the way to the Sudan and Tunisia. He also conquers Israel proper.

But he gets wind of a conspiracy to unseat him, and withdraws his army to Israel where he prepares to engage new enemies. And it is there that the prophetic clock runs out. The end is not even defined for us properly in the 12th chapter of Daniel.

But there are some things that we can glean from this description. A closer look will give us some clues as to the nature of the third kingdom.

First, the kingdom is located between the kingdoms of the south king and the north king. And since he strikes at the south king by taking northeast Africa, *the third king is ruler over the Middle East minus Israel*. The people he persecutes in verses 31 through 36 cannot just be Jews, because other than Jerusalem he is not in control of Israel. Therefore, he is persecuting *all* people of Abrahamic faith.

Finally, we can know from verses 36 through 39 that this man is not a Muslim. Instead, he will boast that he is greater than all of the gods of the region, including the Allah and the God of Abraham.

One last note; it is apparent that the three kings here are not described by what we in Christianity have traditionally described as "the Beast." Chapter seven of Daniel clearly tells us the Beast rules the whole earth, while it is the individual rulers who are represented by the horns. Thus, the third king is just the ruler of three of the horns. Scripture tells us that the new ruler takes over three of the horns for himself, making him first among equals. But his influence is clearly limited as the surrounding kingdoms turn on him. He does become a quasi-religious figure in Revelation, it appears that even there limits exist to the power of this leader.

This is a far cry from the pabulum that usually serves as Christian "end-times" doctrine. It is really straightforward—in the end times, a socio-governmental system will conquer the whole world, dividing the planet into ten regions. There is a wide swath from central Africa to western China that is rich in resources, and apparently some of the regional leaders begin to compete for those resources militarily.

But a new leader, the most powerful and charismatic one of them all, is installed in the area of the Middle East and he soon begins to threaten the resources of his neighbors through expansion. A counterattack is launched by some of the other regions, and thus the table is set for the end of days.

Now, let's switch over to Revelation to get a better look at this prophecy. Let's begin in chapter thirteen. The beast at the beginning of chapter thirteen seems to be the same beast found in chapter 17. Now we get to see why this beast is so worshipped. Apparently he and one of his henchmen can perform miracles.

Further, we know that he rebuilds Babylon as his capital in chapter 17 and it is destroyed in Chapter 18 of Revelation. But this is no Islamic state. Babylon is called "Mother of All Prostitutes and Obscenities in the world" (vs. 5). This hardly describes the tenants of Islam.

In chapter 11 of Daniel we ended with the third king placing his troops in Israel. Verse 44 tells us he will be worried about news from the east and from the north. Revelation 16:12 explains his fears; the "kings of the east" cross the Euphrates River with massive armies. Apparently, chapter 18 shows us that the kings of the east destroy Babylon as they pass by.

It is than that God intervenes in Revelation chapter 19, and the combined armies attempt to turn on God in verse 19, but to no avail; it is over. And still there is no sign of the Islamic or Christian faiths.

I believe that is because Islam and Christianity are no more at this point. The rise of the beast marks the end of Islam and Christianity, not the Final Battle. Scripture is clear in both the new and Old Testament that those who remain worship the Beast, and that all others are crushed beneath its feet.

So is the Beast a man or a state? Or is it a culture? It is all of the above—it is the philosophy of modern humanism. The Beast technically is the entire creature of Revelation and Daniel. However, the charismatic third king appears to the popular representative of the whole, a leader worshipped the whole world wide as the messiah.

But the beast of Revelation is not a person per se. It is obvious from chapter 17 that the beast is a political system in which the horns cooperate. And the woman sitting on the back of the beast is a separate entity destroyed in verse 16 of that chapter. But here's the fascinating part; most versions of the Bible say the woman rules *over* the kingdoms of the earth in verse 18, but that is not quite how it reads in the Greek.

In the Greek, it actually reads that the woman has a kingdom *among* the kings of the earth. That woman is not religious—she is drunk on the blood of the saints in verse 6, and in verse 2 we are told the people of the earth became drunk from the wine of her sexual sins.

So who is the prostitute on the beast? She is the modern Godless, narcissistic, party-hard culture that America is fully enwrapped in and is exporting around the world. The picture in chapter 17 of Revelation is one of an alliance between this culture and the evil kingdom of humanism that comes to power as a result. It is that unholy alliance which is being forged right now, during our lifetimes, and it is our deadliest enemy. Left unchecked it will destroy us.

For those of us who are Christians and Muslims, we must face the stark reality that there is nowhere for us in these passages. The rise of the Beast is the end of our influence upon our prospective nations. Only the Jews will remain, and they only remain as a target that allows God to draw in all humanity for destruction.

This is not direct proof of lack of faith on the earth, that is true. But there are other statements that reinforce this idea. In Luke chapter 18, Jesus tells his disciples the story of a harsh judge and a widow who gets justice from him by her persistence. He goes on to say that God will not deny his children swift justice. But then Jesus adds a peculiar statement in verse 8; "But when I, the son of Man, return, how many will I find who have faith?"

This statement points directly to the great silence of the Bible concerning people of faith other than the Jews. It appears the prophesies of the Bible start at the point of our destruction. This is supported by II Thessalonians chapter 2. This passage clearly spells out that prior to the end of days there will be a great rebellion against God. Furthermore, verse 7 says, "For this lawlessness is already at work secretly…"

It is that rebellion we struggle against as people of faith, whether we are in Jerusalem, Israel or Tehran, Iran or Pittsburgh, Pennsylvania. Our goal is the same; to work against the forces of lawlessness that threaten our destruction. We have been foolish; it doesn't matter if we want to live in an Islamic state in Afghanistan or have a nativity scene or menorah in public in California, our goals are the same, for all of us. We want to help shape the character of our people and affect the government for good.

The kicker is it appears that Christianity and Islam are part of a barrier erected by God as a firewall to protect humanity against this encroaching rebellion. The terrifying reality of the situation is that we are already failing at our divine mission.

We cannot afford to fail. We are like the rock planted by the ocean that holds back the waves. Ultimately, the waves will be broken upon our three faiths, or the waves will break us. The real question is whether we are willing to surrender our children to unspeakable evil and suffering for our failures. If we are, then we should abandon our faiths now. If we are not, we must learn to fight back far more efficiently than we now do. It is time for us to be much more cunning than we have been.

Now that I have established the theological impetus for Islam, Christianity, and Judaism to cooperate together, let's turn our attention to more pressing matters. We have an enemy who is at war with us. If the scriptures are correct, we should be able to trace this rebellion down through the centuries.

So let us turn our attention towards history, and see if we can follow the growth of our enemies over time. In doing so, we will see that the enemy has a strategy for our destruction. And we will see that God has placed us in a perfect position to fight back, if only we will take advantage of our opportunities.

Chapter Two
The New Religion

"I am attacking God, all gods, anything and everything
supernatural, wherever they have been or will be invented."
-Richard Dawkins, *The God Delusion*.

Today we are in the midst of a great
religious war. It is not fought in the sands of Iraq
or the mountains of Afghanistan; instead, it is
fought in iPods and televisions, movies and
discos all around the world. It is a religion of
hatred and intolerance, and millions have been
destroyed to appease it. It is humanism.

The lie told by the humanists about the
Church is that it was the all-powerful, evil,
wicked force of the middle ages that held
humanity down. The truth is that after the fall of
Rome it took centuries for the new barbaric
conquerors of Europe to learn to be civilized, and
Islam and the Church protected the seeds of
knowledge that eventually led to modern Europe.

But don't hold your breath waiting for any gratitude. You certainly will not hear this taught in any classroom in the West.

While the reformation was a necessary process of development as Europe nations began to restructure their governments, it nevertheless did incredible damage to the power of religion in Europe. Luther was correct to point out the excesses of Rome, but he did not stop there. The road to hell is indeed paved with good intentions, and Luther laid the first brick by choosing to stress the centrality of the individual (1). He even took the first small steps towards the acceptance of divorce in the Church (2).

Over time, the fractured Churches in Europe began to lose their power. As the Churches waned and nations waxed stronger, an intellectual movement began which eventually became known as humanism. For our purposes, humanism will simply be described as the belief that humans are the highest moral authority in existence.

By the time Luther nailed his now-famous theses to the door, the foundation for modern totalitarianism was already laid. In 1516, Sir Thomas More published *Utopia*, a wildly successful book that both made him one of the most powerful men in England and ensured that one day his head would be stuck on a spear for all to see. In an ironic fit of idiocy the Catholic Church would canonize him in 1935.

The short tome that is *Utopia* is one of the very first instances in which the basic ideas of communism are put forth in a more or less organized manner. Work is shared. Every family rotates homes by lot, leaving the one in which they were living behind every ten years. There are no locks on the doors, because possessions are not considered private property. There is free and generous health care. Even meals are communal, and people are looked down on for eating in their own homes. Lowly positions that require base instincts such as butchery are left to the people in society that are less than the "good" Utopians.

What makes *Utopia* important is that it promoted the idea that a perfect or near-perfect society can be created. Humanism simply says that to build this better society people must be free to reorganize in new ways. Eventually, the existing governmental, social, and economic structures must be reshaped to these new ideals. It is this search for a real-life utopia that would nearly destroy the world during the 20th century and one day will—maybe sooner than we think.

And that is why humanists hate the Church; not only is the Church one of the most powerful of the traditional social structures, but it flies in the face of utopian ideals by declaring humans are not perfectible. According to the Church, we are all fallen creatures who cannot do good solely through our own will. We need rules to help us and guide our actions. But most importantly, we claim that there is a moral authority above man, and humanists despise the thought.

Here then is the classical socialist claim about society; that people are basically good, and that goodness can run society through socialism. That the distribution of goods and service equally stops greed and other moral failures from occurring. And that those who resist the socialist system or who do not live up to these lofty ideals must be intellectually deficient.

This is the germ of what has become a worldwide war against faith. Humanists portray believers as weak and religion as a crutch. And if the last century was any indication, they are willing to destroy the whole world to make their pie-in-the-sky ideas work. They hate people of faith for the reason that we burst their rancid hallucinations of creating a perfect society.

While these ideas were popular enough at the time that More wrote *Utopia* and became a close adviser of Henry VIII, his ideas were not workable at the time. Socialists claim that it was the Church in Rome that kept the fairy tale from being fulfilled sooner, but this is not true. In reality, governments were not advanced enough at the time to carry out such advanced economic and social functions even on a local level.

When the Germanic and Central European tribes finally started crossing the borders of the Roman Empire to stay, they were not replacing one well-developed nation with another. These were *barbarians*, and they did not have a senate or an emperor or a body of laws or a well-organized society. The vast majority of them could not read even at a rudimentary level. It literally took hundreds of years until Charlemagne finally **began** to build the first state in the west, the Carolingian empire.

So for the decades preceding and following Thomas More the poison of socialism was slowly developed and spread in the West until the time was ripe for the birth of the new humanist religion. That event finally occurred during the French Revolution of the late 1700's.

In the intervening years, the nature of humanism had changed. In *Utopia* religious belief was still external to the state, only completely docile. Most early humanists based their moral ideals on Christian morals and on the ideas of classical literature (3). But the humanists of the enlightenment had a different idea altogether.

The new ideas placed into society through the Reformation and philosophers such as Spinoza started a revolution in human thought. Europe began to split between those who rejected the idea of God and the pious (4). The quickly maturing humanism had totally different ideas about the nature of man. While the Church held that man was in a fallen state, Locke claimed that humans were not born with a sense of right or wrong, or internal principles (5). Respublica Literatura was centered on the idea of "freedom" and personal development which would somehow make people "more human" (6).

By 1700, skepticism was an important philosophy in the movement, further undercutting religious principle. Leaders of the Enlightenment held that reason alone was sufficient to solve life's issues (7). God was no longer central to the equation.

But that is not to say the leaders of the movement wanted to do away with religion; they had plans for it of their own, which they would carry out during the French Revolution. In the minds of the French Revolutionaries, worship would belong to the state and the state alone— and the state would have no other gods before it.

Under the influence of the leaders of the Enlightenment the idea of sacredness was attached to civic ideals rather than to religious practice (8). Service to the state was promoted as the highest good (9). Basically the new religion would be one in which the people would be worshipping themselves, in proxy through the state (10). Religion would no longer turn outwards, focusing on higher moral principle.

Now it would be turned inwards, focusing on the here and now. The French Revolutionaries believed all actions were public in nature (11).

The state itself would become the locus of the public will. Rousseau had promoted the idea of the general will of the people (12) and the Revolutionaries would incorporate that idea into the new religion. The central document of the Revolution, the "Declaration of the Rights of Man and Citizen" written in 1789 contained the following statement in declaration #6; "Law is the expression of the general will…" (13). The first dictator of the new "Republic", Robespierre, said that "the people" were more important than the individual (14). This principle of the whole over the individual would be a central tenant to all of the totalitarian ideologies of the 20th century right up to the present. Rousseau, through the influence of his writing in support of these ideas, became the father of totalitarianism (15).

Immediately this new religion of the state declared war against the Church. Rousseau intended to replace Christianity with a "civil religion" (16), and the French Revolutionaries would accept this call to battle. Robespierre began the process of organizing state religious practices in 1794, just two days before the Terror began (17).

Revolutionary leaders persecuted the Catholic Church to the point that even clerical robes were outlawed (18). The peasant uprising that was meant to secure "liberty, fraternity, equality" led instead to the first fascist state and the first modern dictatorships instead (19). France became a terror state, persecuting it enemies violently, both real and imagined. By the time Napoleon restored order in 1800 over 100,000 thousand Frenchmen had been slaughtered, most simply to satisfy the unchecked imagination of those who had gone mad on power (20).

But this was only the beginning. The death that the French Revolutionaries brought with the guillotine was only a trickle compared to what others would unleash later. Over the next century, Christianity would be replaced by the new humanist religion throughout Europe (21). It would even gain a foothold in the United States under the guise of "Progressivism".

Next we will look at America to better understand where America is today and why. The seeds of the current political environment were sown at the time the first settlers set foot on North America. They came to build a better life for themselves, but eventually would be torn apart by the great moral issue of the time, slavery.

Along the way they inadvertently created not one nation, but two. Those two nations first clashed over slavery but have continued to struggle against one another ever since. It is that struggle which is at the heart of America.

1. Thompson, Stephen P., ED. Turning Points in World History: The Reformation. Greenhaven Press, 1999. Page 73.

2. Thompson, Stephen P., ED. Turning Points in World History: The Reformation. Greenhaven Press, 1999. Page 164.

3. Thompson, Stephen P., ED. Turning Points in World History: The Reformation. Greenhaven Press, 1999. Page 80.

4. Reitbergen, Peter. Europe: a Cultural History. Routledge, 1998. Page 311.

5. Reitbergen, Peter. Europe: a Cultural History. Routledge, 1998. Page 308.

6. Reitbergen, Peter. Europe: a Cultural History. Routledge, 1998. Page 285.

7. Popkin, Richard. The Columbia History of Western Philosophy. Columbia University Press, 1999. Page 462.

8. Chartier, Roger, Trans. by Lydia G. Cochrane. The Cultural Origins of the French Revolution. Duke University Press, 1991. Page 109.

9. Reitbergen, Peter. Europe: a Cultural History. Routledge, 1998. Page 315.

10. Goldberg, Jonah. Liberal Fascism. Doubleday, 2007. Page 39.

11. Chartier, Roger, Trans. by Lydia G. Cochrane. The Cultural Origins of the French Revolution. Duke University Press, 1991. Page 196.

12. Goldberg, Jonah. Liberal Fascism. Doubleday, 2007. Page 39.

13. Reitbergen, Peter. Europe: a Cultural History. Routledge, 1998. Page 338.

14. Goldberg, Jonah. Liberal Fascism. Doubleday, 2007. Page 38.

15. Goldberg, Jonah. Liberal Fascism. Doubleday, 2007. Page 38.

16. Himmelfarb, Gertrude. One Nation, Two Cultures. Alfred A. Knopf, 1999. Page 104.

17. Himmelfarb, Gertrude. One Nation, Two Cultures. Alfred A. Knopf, 1999. Page 105.

18. Goubert, Pierre. The Course of French History. Franklin Watts, Inc., 1988 (English version). Page 304.

19. Goldberg, Jonah. Liberal Fascism. Doubleday, 2007. Pages 12-13.

20. Goubert, Pierre. The Course of French History. Franklin Watts, Inc., 1988 (English version). Page 314.

21. Chartier, Roger, Trans. by Lydia G. Cochrane. The Cultural Origins of the French Revolution. Duke University Press, 1991. Page 92.

Chapter Three
The Two Americas

"If we do not hang together we shall all hang separately."
-Benjamin Franklin.

Among the most basic claims of the fundamentalist Muslims is that America does not have the moral authority to lead the other nations of the world. This claim is based on the changes that have occurred in American society over the last hundred years, and it is in fact correct. For reasons I will discuss later American society does indeed lack the moral basis for world leadership.

What most people outside the United States may not know—and what the vast majority of Americans themselves do not know--is that America has always been this way. The dirty little secret about the United States is that there are in reality two Americas, and there has been ever since colonial times.

The history of the United States is really the history of the conflict between these two groups. And the history of my country may be broken down into one simple idea; the right side may have won the battles, but the wrong side won the argument.

Of course, the average American history book will tiptoe around these truths for the most part, but you must know how this came about in order to understand the nature of the conflict in which we are involved. American culture as it currently practiced is a perverse mixture of these two separate cultures.

The same factors which changed Europe were at work in the British colonies of North America during their settlement. The economic boom of the 17th century and the increased rejection of faith that occurred during that period combined to produce the America in which I live as I write theses words.

Economically speaking, the British were intelligent enough to realize that they had been lucky when the Spanish Armada was destroyed in 1588. They were also observant enough to realize that it was the incredible economic growth of Spain which made assembling the armada possible in the first place. And that economic growth came from Spain's American colonies.

For example, the mines at Potosi produced a staggering amount of silver before 1650 (1). The other nations of Europe could not afford to allow Spain to outgrow them economically. From the very beginnings of modern Europe it was recognized that economic power equaled military power. The advent of the Armada made it clear to the English they could not afford to let themselves be outdone.

Yet the conquest and administration of two distant continents could not be carried out by any single European nation with the technology available at the time. That is why both the Spanish and British allotted use of the new territories to private enterprises. Britain granted the Virginia Charter in 1606 and a year later the

first successful colony was founded at
Jamestown. Later, the northern colonies would
be settled.

The problem was, and is, that the two
colonies were settled for completely different
reasons, and it was the internal motivations of the
two regions that eventually brought them to
blows. While the two groups of colonies would
shake off British rule eventually, they were far
more different than they were alike.

In New England the motivation was
religious. There, it was the social climate of
Europe that drove the settlers to cross the
Atlantic. Europe was going through its first
serious spate of religious persecution during the
time of the Pilgrims and the Puritans.

There had been some religious
persecution before, but usually it had been
directed against the Jews, such as in Spain and
England. But this new round of persecution was
politically motivated, a dangerous precedent that

others would harness for their own purposes with terrifying efficiency later in history.

The Jews were still under the gun, especially in Spain, where they were seen as traitors who were the cause of military setbacks such as the defeat of the Spanish at Pernambuco in 1630 (2). But they did not migrate to America in large enough numbers to establish their own colony. It was the immigration of several Christian sects from northern Europe that set the New England colonies apart from their southern neighbors.

These new settlers were doing more than merely fleeing persecution, but their mistreatment certainly helped push them out the door, so to speak. The common propaganda taught about the first settlers of the New England area is that they immigrated to the New World to find "freedom" to practice their religion. That is a lie. The paramount motivation for the northern settlers was to form a moral society overseen by a moral government at the local level (3). From the beginning Biblical law was a part of the legal code in Massachusetts (4). In 1628 Thomas Merton and his group was forced to abandon their settlement at Merriemount due to their conflicts with their neighbors over their lascivious behavior (5).

The Pilgrims who landed at Pilgrim Rock in 1620 were soon followed by the Puritans who founded Massachusetts in 1629. The Puritans did come to New England specifically to flee a new round of persecution (6). They were followed by the Quakers in 1657 (7). In 1681, Pennsylvania was founded by William Penn.

Even the Anglicans of Britain began to see the New World as an opportunity to create a better society although somewhat lukewarmly (8). Still, the Northern Colonies surged forward economically and were even in population with the Southern Colonies by about 1650 (9).

The southern Colonies were different; they were founded through land grants that were meant to be business ventures based on trade

(10). Émigrés were paid for their transport which they worked off on arrival. Economic profits were the main motivation for the Southern Colonies and they focused their energies on exports to England. In contrast the Northern Colonies developed their own local economies and as a result were much less dependent on imported goods throughout the colonial period (11).

This focus on profit in the southern colonies meant that they were far less developed culturally and socially. The strong local governments of the Northern Colonies simply did not exist in the South. Over time, the Southern Colonies began to import more and more slaves, which would eventually become the defining issue of the young country. And it wasn't just slaves that were shipped to the south; criminals were also imported in quantity.

The settlement of Carolina was a particularly lawless affair, except for the express right granted to hold slaves (12). That was one law which would stand for almost 200 years and solely be retained for economic reasons. Originally it was the Germanic tribal idea of "others" that allowed the ownership of slaves to begin in the southern colonies (13). But nationalistic tribalism was slowly giving way to modern colonialism, and it is this movement that would allow the continued ownership of slaves in the Southern Colonies.

So let's take a moment to review the philosophies that drove the colonial period. Those ideas are still with us today, and recognizing them are of critical importance. Those same arguments shape the American political landscape today.

The first thing to understand is that colonialism derived from the idea of imperialism, and imperialism was in fact a cultural phenomenon. This is so much true that I will refer to the current imperial impulse of the West, in particular America, as Cultural Imperialism, because that is the real nature of what has happened over the last few decades and is still happening now.

Cultural imperialism is a large part of what drives modern humanism and is central to the diplomacy and strategies of the West in other nations, especially in Muslim countries. It was developed from the Germanic tribalism that dominated the middle ages. The tribes that penetrated the old Roman Empire did so as independent groups that stamped their own identities on the areas where they settled. And they saw themselves as independent of their neighbors.

But as the economic power of the West expanded, modern nations began to develop. When those nations realized that they were more militarily and economically powerful than the other nation of the world, that sense of separateness became a sense of superiority. That was translated into Imperialism, the idea that it was OK to conquer less advanced nations. It was also that sense of superiority which later gave birth to the phenomenon of Cultural Imperialism, the belief that the nations of the West were justified in subjugating and dominating less advanced cultures.

Further, Europeans began to believe they had the right to impose western culture on less advanced peoples in other nations. Much of this has been blamed on the missionary work of the Church. But this is only partly true. The Bible does not provide cultural direction, only moral and spiritual guidance. Nor is there any sense of culture in the Bible outside of the community of believers. And even this is not well developed. It appears that God is far less concerned with how we consecrate a marriage than He is that we do not cheat on our spouses. Of course European missionaries did not recognize this as they proselytized; no one from the West did at the time.

But for a brief, shining moment the Northern Colonies began to live out the ideas of social morality. Even priests of the Anglican

Church believed that the Northern Colonies presented an opportunity to build a better society (14). The leaders of the Massachusetts colony were elected by Church members (15), and moral laws were publicly upheld. Many towns in New England kept lists of drunks, for example (16).

These deep differences led to friction between the northern and southern Colonies. The growing conflict between the two sets of colonies eventually became somewhat of a propaganda war. When Rhode Island was formed, the new colony found their Puritan neighbors despised their liberal constitution (17). The northerners even went so far as to call the Dutch and Virginian settlers "Egyptians" (18).

Left to their own devices, the northern and southern colonies would probably never have joined forces. But London felt the need to better control the huge economic resources of her colonies more closely. Except for British blundering and ineptitude there might never have been a United States.

In many ways, the ideas of those early secular leaders of Europe mirrored those of modern liberals. Secularists have always coveted economic power over other forms, and this impetus began long before communism. In France, protectionist trade tariffs were instituted in 1667 to protect French Trade from competition (19). The British, anxious to develop their own economy, simply set out to compete on even footing. That meant maximizing the gains they could get from their new colonies.

The chess match between the Colonists and England began in 1624, when political control of the colonies was transferred to Britain. The territories were broken into Royal Provinces, and this would become the main sticking point between the colonists and London. By 1700, all of the American colonies were led by governors instead of by local governments (20).

The colonists moved to organize themselves, ostensibly to protect themselves from the natives (21). It is doubtful that the colonists had any other intentions, but the practice of continental diplomacy would pay dividends as the conflict between the colonies and the mother country would grow into open battle.

In the end, that alliance between the Northern and Southern Colonies would be too fragile to be maintained. At first the friction between the two Americas would lead to armed conflict between the states, later to be replaced by the social conflict that divides America today. But for a brief time, less than a hundred years, it appeared as if America might become the locus for a truly moral society.

Over time those hopes would prove to be an illusion.

1. Kamen, Henry. Empire; How Spain Became a World Power 1492-1763. HarperCollins Publishers, 2003. Page 286.

2. Kamen, Henry. Empire; How Spain Became a World Power 1492-1763. HarperCollins Publishers, 2003. Page 344.

3. Meining, D.W. The Shaping of America. Yale University Press, 1986. Page 105.

4. McDougall, Walter. Freedom Just Around the Corner: A New American History 1585-1828. HarperCollins 2004. Page 59.

5. McDougall, Walter. Freedom Just Around the Corner: A New American History 1585-1828. HarperCollins 2004. Page 54.

6. Fraser, Rebecca. The History of Britain. W.W. Norton & Company, Inc., 2003. Page 325.

7. Meining, D.W. The Shaping of America. Yale University Press, 1986. Page 93.

8. Quinn, David Beers. England and the Discovery of America 1481-1620. Alfred A. Knopf, 1973. Page 361.

9. McDougall, Walter. Freedom Just Around the Corner: A New American History 1585-1828. HarperCollins 2004. Page 69.

10. Meining, D.W. The Shaping of America. Yale University Press, 1986. Pages 144-146.

11. McDougall, Walter. Freedom Just Around the Corner: A New American History 1585-1828. HarperCollins 2004. Page 63.

12. McDougall, Walter. Freedom Just Around the Corner: A New American History 1585-1828. HarperCollins 2004. Pages 77-78.

13. McDougall, Walter. Freedom Just Around the Corner: A New American History 1585-1828. HarperCollins 2004. Page 75.

14. Quinn, David Beers. England and the Discovery of America 1481-1620. Alfred A. Knopf, 1973. Page 361.

15. Furnas, J.C. The Americans: A Social History of the United States 1587-1914. G.P. Putnam's Sons, 1969. Page 65.

16. Furnas, J.C. The Americans: A Social History of the United States 1587-1914. G.P. Putnam's Sons, 1969. Page 65.

17. McDougall, Walter. Freedom Just Around the Corner: A New American History 1585-1828. HarperCollins 2004. Page 65.

18. Furnas, J.C. The Americans: A Social History of the United States 1587-1914. G.P. Putnam's Sons, 1969. Page 71.

19. Goubert, Pierre. The Course of French History. Franklin Watts, Inc., 1988 (English version). Page 193.

20. McDougall, Walter. Freedom Just Around the Corner: A New American History 1585-1828. HarperCollins 2004. Page 95.

21. McDougall, Walter. Freedom Just Around the Corner: A New American History 1585-1828. HarperCollins 2004. Page 68.

Chapter Four
Prophets of the State

"...asceticism and puritanism are virtually indispensable
means of education and ennobling if a race wants to
become master over its origins in the rabble, and work its
way up towards future rule."
-Friedrich Nietzsche, *Beyond Good and Evil*.

In the early 1800's the new religion of
statism spread rapidly into central Europe, fueled
by the grapeshot from Napoleon's cannon. By
the end of the century, Europe would be made up
of an array of nationalist states all of whom were
armed to the teeth. Before the century was out
France herself would be handed an embarrassing
defeat at the hands of the newly-united Germans.

But no one was quite clear on the tenants
of the new religion. It lacked the kind of psychic
force necessary to bind people to it strongly.
That is why once Napoleon was defeated another
humanist state did not rise to take its place until
Bismarck. What the new religion needed was a

prophet capable of organizing the new religion into a dogma that all could follow. Unfortunately for the rest of us, it did not take long for the prophets of the new religion to arise.

It all happened around a single date in time, the most important date in history since the birth of Christ; 1859. That year can be rightly considered year 1 in the Humanist Era. From that single year would spring the philosophies that would set the world on fire in less than a century.

There were four movements that year. *Capital* by Marx and *The Origin of Species* by Darwin would appear; *Tristan and Isolde* would be completed by Wagner; and the arguments of Abraham Lincoln concerning "the Union" would begin spreading their way through America as Lincoln ambled towards the presidency.

By the end of the century, three branches of humanist thought would exist; Communism, Americanism, and Supernationalism. And they would bloody the world. They were all built on the back of another idea, Positivism. Positivism was built around the belief that humans were entering a new scientific age (1). Scientific advancement dazzled the people of the West, "proving" the power of materialism and science (2). Many argued that very soon, science would provide the answers to all of man's problems—not a bit unlike the nonsense liberals parrot today.

These four men stepped into the spotlight of the 19th century, creating the humanist movement we have today. By the time they were finished, the humanist movement would have its own creation myth (Darwin), its own economics (Marx), its own martyr/savior (Lincoln), and even its own music (Wagner). They are considered by humanists the secular equivalent to the trinity, plus an economist for good measure.

There would be a fifth prophet, Nietzsche, who would appear the end of the century, but he would do less to create than to direct the new religion. Nietzsche would codify humanist philosophy through his work, but did not invent it. If he had not been born it would not have mattered as far as the tenants of humanism are concerned.

Arguably the most important of the four is Darwin. His ideas were the only ones accepted across all three branches of humanism— American liberals have never been majority communist, preferring the Fascist economic model instead (more about that later). And Darwin's ideas led directly to a significant amount of the death visited upon the world by humanism.

The rush away from traditional religion and towards the new humanist religion did more than make Darwinism into an accepted scientific theory; it became a worldview (3). Darwin's evolutionary ideas secured the primacy of science in the West (4). Not only was God no longer a necessity, but now it could be proven. Now, humanism could firmly plant its flag in the back of its fellow human beings, because without a God there could be no absolute right or wrong.

However, Darwinist theory would also give birth to a new burst of racism. These evolutionary ideas would serve as the basis for a whole new level of racist thought (5). "Scientific" racism was not new, but Darwinism ensured that it would remain fashionable and acceptable for a long time.

Scientific racism first developed during the enlightenment. Works such as *Natural History of Man* by Leclerć in 1778 and *Essai sur la Physiognomy* in 1781 made scientific racism an acceptable part of the French Revolution. Enlightenment leaders strongly supported these ideas (6). French Revolutionaries even accepted the negative stereotype of the Jews that had been so popular in Europe for so long (7). In 1864, the Anthropological Society of London debated exterminating the "lower" races, Africans in particular (8).

It was on the back of this new "scientific" frontier that Marx offered up his *Capital*. Through that work, and the *Communist Manifesto*

Marx laid out a powerful argument for a mechanical socialism—economic science applied to the state. Contrary to the supernationalists, communism wanted to do away with nationality in exchange for a common economic society (9).

Marx despised the idea of morality (10) and said that communism should abolish religion and morality (11) as well as do away with the family (12). In the place of the old national structure, the state should become the dictatorship of the "working class" (13). But like his brethren, Marx saw not the death of religion but its replacement as imminent, calling communism the "new gospel" (14).

While Europe was on its way to the brink of madness, the advancement of humanist ideas in America was much slower. Distance and time separated Americans from their European brothers, and that greatly slowed their descent. Furthermore, the change occurred later in America, giving rise to a movement that looked and behaved quite differently. It was the beginning of the same process that took place in Europe, but it would take a different turn in America.

And that is why I have placed Lincoln third on the list. While it might be argued that here in America the influence of Lincoln was far greater than in the other countries, it must also be recognized that outside America Lincoln had very little influence. For example, while millions of Americans have become socialists since Marx, scant few foreigners have become federalists since Lincoln.

Yet what Lincoln did would change the face of America forever, for both good and evil. It was under Lincoln that the Presidency first gained its dictatorial war powers; it was Lincoln who suspended habeas corpus, jailed dissidents, and had the first income tax imposed upon the American public (15).

Still, the important part of Lincoln's legacy is not the fact that he managed to do these things, but that he was able to persuade the

American people to accept them. It is *that* process, and the long march it started which led America away from true faith which is the most important part of what happened to American society during the Civil War.

Right from the beginning Americans saw their own future as glorious (16). The American Revolution had been a powerful religious event for the Americans involved (17). Ethan Allen wrote that he fought because he believed he was choosing between freedom and tyranny at the time (18).

These feelings began with the Puritan hopes of building a better society. This quickly developed into an "American Zionism" that we have never fully gotten over. This New Zionism was solidified through the American Revolution (19). After the Revolution was over, American churches scrambled to pledge allegiance to the fledgling Republic (20), and the idol of Americanism was born.

It was not a completely peaceful transformation from Puritanism to Americanism. Some clergy were persecuted and even jailed during the Revolutionary War for their political statements (21). And when it came to politics, George Washington was personally against the Church exercising any influence (22). There was considerable resistance to the completely secular constitution that was adopted, but the founding fathers refused to budge on the issue (23). Some feared "In the beginning, God…" was being replaced by "In the beginning, Thomas Jefferson…" (24), yet that did little to slow the growth of statolatry in America. Over time, America itself would start to become a religious concept (25).

Before Lincoln was elected President this New Zionism began to supercede the traditional American Puritanism for which the Colonies were famous (26). But it was under Lincoln that the transformation from Puritanism to Americanism would be completed (27).

According to David Gelertner (from whom I got the term "American Zionism"), "...Lincoln saw the Republican Party as a new kind of Church" (28).

Thus the Civil War became America's tipping point. Before it, the Church competed with the state for the loyalty of the American public. Afterwards it never would again. As the first pictures trickled back from the American killing fields, something changed in Americans. According to the History Channel, Americans looked at those pictures and agreed with Lincoln that the principles for which they fought were worth the price. After the Civil War, America itself became something to believe in (29). Adding insult to injury was the fact that it was the American Churches which had taken the lead in condemning slavery, just as the Church had done in England.

I do not as some others do doubt that Lincoln had the right to free the slaves; it was his reasoning that was false. To call slavery a moral issue and to say that the Union needed to end slavery due to that moral impulse which was written into the Declaration of Independence would have been perfectly correct. But what Lincoln did was not. Instead of taking a straightforward approach, Lincoln declared in the Gettysburg address that *the principles under which the American government began were above the constitution,* and that is a lie. Even in the Declaration of Independence to which Lincoln so masterfully alluded, the founders declared they were operating according to "…the Laws of Nature and of Nature's God…" getting their rights from the "Creator", not the state.

Instead of establishing the proper order of government—from the Creator and to the people to govern themselves equally thereby--Lincoln chose to follow the humanist pattern developing in Europe that the state exists only to do the "will of the people" regardless of whether that will is right or wrong. Lincoln can rightly be lauded for his insistence on freeing the slaves, which any moral person would do. But he sold America up the river in return, and that has proven to be nearly as toxic as the disease of slavery from which America was cured.

I mention Wagner last, even though in a lot of ways he is the only one of the four to truly have a worldwide presence other than Darwin. No one should ever underestimate the power Wagner has held over the world. It was Wagner who gave the nascent humanist movement its meaning. *Tristan* placed the ideas of humanism into a heroic and powerful and meaningful context.

Tristan was the first truly successful propaganda piece, being based on a medieval "Teutonic" story. It fleshed out the emotions of the time masterfully. Not only that, but many consider *Tristan* to be the seminal work which led to modern music. According to this concept, modern music was the love child of humanist ideology. Every time you hear a hip-hop song degrading women and the value of life, you can thank Wagner. Secular ideas have dominated American music, and it has taken far too long for the Church to begin making inroads into the pop music area.

In nearly every nation on the face of the planet, one can hear some sort of secular music. As I will explain in a future chapter, this is no accident. Humanism has powerfully marketed itself to the whole world through the media, and often both the music and the method are the message. All thanks to one little opera finished in 1859 and not even performed until 1865. Fittingly enough, according to Wikipedia two composers have died while directing the opera, both during the second act.

Strangely enough it is the second act of humanism that would also prove to be the deadliest so far.

1. Barzun, Jacques. Darwin, Marx, Wagner. Doubleday Anchor 1941. Page 49.

2. Barzun, Jacques. Darwin, Marx, Wagner. Doubleday Anchor 1941. Pages 9-10.

3. Barzun, Jacques. Darwin, Marx, Wagner. Doubleday Anchor 1941. Page 52.

4. Barzun, Jacques. Darwin, Marx, Wagner. Doubleday Anchor 1941. Page 65.

5. Weitz, Eric D. Genocide: Utopias of Race and Nation. Princeton University Press
2003. Page 37.

6. Mosse, George L. The Image of Man: The Creation of Modern Masculinity. Oxford Press, 1996. Page 25.

7. Mosse, George L. The Image of Man: The Creation of Modern Masculinity. Oxford Press, 1996. Page 65.

8. Reitbergen, Peter. Europe: a Cultural History. Routledge, 1998. Page 389.

9. Marx, Karl and Friedrich Engels. The Communist Manifesto. Pocket Books 1964. Page 90.

10. Barzun, Jacques. Darwin, Marx, Wagner. Doubleday Anchor 1941. Page 177.

11. Marx, Karl and Friedrich Engels. The Communist Manifesto. Pocket Books 1964. Page 92.

12. Marx, Karl and Friedrich Engels. The Communist Manifesto. Pocket Books 1964. Pages 87-88.

13. Barzun, Jacques. Darwin, Marx, Wagner. Doubleday Anchor 1941. Page 163.

14. Marx, Karl and Friedrich Engels. The Communist Manifesto. Pocket Books 1964. Page 113.

15. DiLorenzo, Thomas J. Lincoln's 'Second American Revolution'.
http://www.lewrockwell.com/dilorenzo/dilorenzo32.html

16. Stiles, TJ. In Their Own Words: Founding Fathers. Berkley Publishing Group 1999. Page xxiv.

17. McDougall, Walter. Freedom Just Around the Corner: A New American History 1585-1828. HarperCollins 2004. Page 237.

18. Stiles, TJ. In Their Own Words: Founding Fathers. Berkley Publishing Group 1999. Pages 76-77.

19. Gelertner, David. Americanism: The Fourth Great Western Religion. Doubleday 2007. Page 74.

20. McDougall, Walter. Freedom Just Around the Corner: A New American History 1585-1828. HarperCollins 2004. Pages 323-328.

21. Church, Forrest. So Help Me God. Harcourt 2007. Page 5.

22. Church, Forrest. So Help Me God. Harcourt 2007. Page 3.

23. Anderson, Dr. C. Thomas and Don Evevoldsen. Me My Country My God. Winword Publishing. Pages 209-210.

24. Church, Forrest. So Help Me God. Harcourt 2007. Page 1.

25. McDougall, Walter. Freedom Just Around the Corner:
A New American History 1585-1828. HarperCollins 2004.
Page 209.

26. Gelertner, David. Americanism: The Fourth Great
Western Religion. Doubleday 2007. Page 75.

27. Gelertner, David. Americanism: The Fourth Great
Western Religion. Doubleday 2007. Pages 103-104.

28. Gelertner, David. Americanism: The Fourth Great
Western Religion. Doubleday 2007. Page 115.

29. Gelertner, David. Americanism: The Fourth Great
Western Religion. Doubleday 2007. Page 154.

Chapter Five
The Dark Time

"I would conquer the stars if I could."
-British Explorer Cecil Rhodes.

By 1900, all of the forces were in place that would lead to the destruction of the 20th century. At this point, humanism was dividing into three parts. First were the communists and socialists, who were mostly internationalists, and especially strong in Europe. In America, the progressives were the mainstream, with their focus on social and technological progress, led by Teddy Roosevelt and Woodrow Wilson. Finally, the fascists competed in Europe with the communists, offering the blessings of supernationalism to its followers.

In the late 1800's Nietzsche gave this all one final push forward, promising all who partook glory unlimited for their efforts. "…life

as such is will to power…" he whispered (1).
Nietzsche would become the great humanist
prophet of the future during the turn of the
century. He called morality "a piece of tyranny"
against both nature and reason (2). According to
Nietzsche, "To our strongest drive, the tyrant in
us, not only our reason but also our conscience
submit" (3).

The important part of Nietzsche is not that
he declared God dead in *Thus Spoke Zarathustra*.
His contribution to the humanist movement lies
in his giving it legitimacy. No one in any of the
three movements pointed to Nietzsche as the first
source of their beliefs, but they all pointed to
Nietzsche for confirmation of their principles.

And religion was always at the point of
his attack. He called Jewish morality a "slave
revolt in morals". Nietzsche called Christianity
"the most fatal kind of self-presumption ever",
leading to "…a shrunken, almost ludicrous
species, a herd animal, something full of good

will, sickly and mediocre…the European of today" (4).

Nietzsche made it OK for humanism to pop the cork and do evil. In fact, Nietzsche never recognized evil at all; "The greatest epochs of our life are the occasions when we gain the courage to rebaptize our evil qualities as our best qualities" (5). To Nietzsche, the struggle of life was all there was. "Few are made for independence—it is a privilege of the strong" (6).

Yet Nietzsche was not without his tender mercies; "One has been a bad spectator of life if one has not also seen the hand that in a considerate fashion—kills" (7). Hitler could not have said it better. Now, with no God to answer to and no conscience to bother with, humanism would become a plague upon the land.

The nations that entered World War I were driven by the same impulses that led Japan and Germany to start World War II. These were not aberrations; they were the natural outcomes to Western culture (8). America's defeat of

Spain in 1898 transformed her into a major power as well. The stage was set for bloodshed on an unprecedented scale.

This toxic humanist mixture took over in the West, becoming an unstoppable force. The Assassination of Duke Ferdinand created the excuse for the pent-up forces of humanism to be unleashed. So on August 7, British and French troops invaded the German colony of Togoland, beginning the 30-year struggle for the soul of the whole world. That battle for supremacy would change everything.

Those humanist forces, compressed like a spring, exploded onto the unsuspecting world during the two great wars of the twentieth century. The First World War led to the rise of communism in Russia in 1917 and the rise of fascism in Italy six years later. America would be caught in the middle of the struggle between these two versions of socialism until the 1930's, unable to decide which side it preferred.

Both sides continued the war on faith, but in different ways. As Dmitri Volkogonov put it, "The Leninist version of Marxism was made flesh in this great country, becoming something like a secular religion in the process" (9). Lenin was an atheist who saw traditional religion as a form of oppression, (10) a view still widely held today among humanists.

Lenin demanded the separation of the Church and state in 1905 (11) and put his beliefs into action quickly upon taking power. On February 23, 1922 orders were issued by Lenin to remove all valuables from the Russian Churches (12). Under Lenin's reign of terror Church leaders were murdered regularly (13). By 1937, the Church was all but destroyed (14).

Yet the bloodletting did not let up; after the 12 million casualties of WWI, another 13 million died in the civil war under Lenin (15). In 1921-22 alone, there were 25 million people in Russia who were starving (16). Russia became a police state as Lenin consolidated power, (17) and the darkness of humanism began to settle across the land.

At the end of the First World War, America was also teetering on the brink. The progressive President Woodrow Wilson was busy building on the foundation laid by Lincoln concerning the power of the Presidency during wartime. In a lot of ways, Wilson was a traditional liberal who saw the classic racist movie "Birth of a Nation" and approved (18). And he did irreparable harm to American society in two ways.

To start with, Wilson was America's first dictator. He did this legally, just as Hitler would in 1933, through legislation. Two bills were passed and signed in a few days in 1918, and when they were enacted, Woodrow Wilson literally had unlimited power. The first bill was signed by Wilson on May 16, and was called the Espionage Act. For all intents and purposes, it eliminated freedom of speech and the press (19).

The second was signed four days later on May 20, and was aptly named the Overman Act.

The Overman Act literally gave Wilson an unchecked ability to operate the United States government by executive command for the remainder of the war plus six months. And the bill specifically stated that *any* law that interfered with Wilson's ability to do so was null and void (20). The Constitution, Bill of Rights, local and state laws—all would be null and void under the bill if they interfered with the President's activities.

But even worse was the mob mentality that developed which closely resembled later totalitarian states in Europe. An unruly organization of regular citizens sprung up under the American Protective League, (21) and they simply went around enforcing mob rule. They went to the same excesses seen in other totalitarian states, terrorizing the regular population at large (22). Just as during the Revolutionary War, Ministers were acceptable targets (23). People were even murdered by these thugs, and nothing was done most of the time. There were times when living under Wilson was worse than living under Mussolini (24).

Fortunately, Wilson realized that trying to establish a permanent dictatorship would provoke too much resistance. After the war America pretty much went back to business as usual. The dictatorship was allowed to lapse on the given date and Wilson left the White House on schedule.

By the time Wilson left office fascism was already on the rise in Europe. Mussolini was originally an experienced socialist who had been very involved in the communist party in Italy by the beginning of the war. His father was a devout socialist himself who served on the First International with Marx and Engels and read to Mussolini from *Das Capital* when he was a child (25). Early in his career Lenin admired Mussolini and spoke well of him (26).

Like communism, fascism was part of a worldwide movement to replace classical government and social structures, including the Church (27). Mussolini was viciously anti-Christian (28) who declared fascism itself a form of religion (29). While communism simply removed religion, fascism supplanted it.

Fascism and communism are both forms of socialism, but there are important differences. Communism works off of the idea of direct state control of the economy. Communist society was built around social communalism, as was fascism to a point. The picture from *Utopia* of everyone in the community eating in the same mess hall was actually practiced at times in China during the "cultural revolution" of the 60's.

Fascism practiced control of the economy and business but usually not direct ownership, in practical terms more corporatist than communist. And while there were leanings towards social communalism it was much less prevalent in fascism. Instead of the worker, the state was the center of society under fascism. Much like the supernationalists, fascists saw the state as savior. It was Mussolini who termed the phrase "totalitarianism", where everything was a part of the state, and there was nothing outside of it (30).

President Wilson was very much cut from the same cloth as Mussolini. Wilson opposed individual rights and disparaged the constitution (31). The goal of American progressives was not to promote true democracy but to produce middle-class dependence on the state (32). It was hoped that World War I would make the American people more dependent on the government (33).

Under Wilson, the state gained some real power. For example criticizing the government got you jail time. During the First World War, over 175,000 Americans went to prison simply for disagreeing with government policy (34).

This was also the time that public school systems were strengthened throughout the West, especially in America. Just like in the Europe,

American progressives created public schools to help replace the family, not for educational purposes (35). Both fascism and communism assaulted the traditional role of the family in the culture (36).

Communists eventually wanted the state to take over all the functions of the home, even the laundry, while leaders such as Alexandra Kollontai promoted the takeover of parental functions as well (37). Hitler placed explicit obligations on the youth of Germany to the state (38).

Such ideas were also experimented with under President Wilson. The first concerted attempts to indoctrinate children began under Wilson and with his approval (39). During World War I, children were even encouraged to eat less by signing pledges and through nursery rhymes (40).

Even today, education is mainly used for indoctrination and socialistic purposes. That is why today Islamic children in Italy are forced into a scholastic ghetto, (41) just as liberals do to black children in America. Despite all the complaints, Western schools do exactly what they were designed to do—indoctrinate. As some very wise men I know recently wrote, "Most of what you need to know to be successful in life and to be a responsible citizen will not come from the classroom" (42). It never did.

The similarities between Mussolini and Wilson undoubtedly helped make fascism very popular in America during the 20's and popular it was (43). Mussolini (followed by Lenin) topped a 1927 survey of great men conducted by Literary Digest (44). Will Rogers, Sigmund Freud, and Winston Churchill were also among the early Mussolini supporters (45). American journalists loved Mussolini as well (46).

It was the coming of Hitler and Roosevelt that finally broke the spell. Hitler because Nazism was completely Germanocentric and racist, and Roosevelt because he was drawn to communism and not fascism. Of all the humanist movements, none was more poisonous to religion than Nazism. The Germans warred with religion on two fronts, not just when it came to the destruction of the Jews.

Hitler and the Nazis spoke very little about the Jews except in terms of their connection with communism. Just like Muslims today, the Jews of Europe in the early part of the century lived in their own communities and kept their own customs. This made it easy to create the rumors that would turn Jews into the enemy of the state. The main two charges can still be heard on the left today, that Jews run the media and the international banking system. But you can read these modern American liberal thoughts in *Mein Kampf*. While it is true that the Nazis saw the Jews and blacks as lesser races, the truth is Hitler saw the Jews as the perpetrators of Marxism and the people who run the international banking system and media in order to enslave the world, and as we shall see those kinds of beliefs are still popular today.

Hitler's relationship to the rest of the world is not so clear—no one is anxious to hurry up and claim him as one of their own. Nevertheless, it is clear that just like the other fascist states, Nazism was a form of socialism. More than adequate evidence can be found for this at http://jonjayray.tripod.com/hitler.html and in the book *Liberal Fascism* by Jonah Goldberg, so I will not repeat it here. Neither will I argue about whether the Holocaust occurred; the Army footage from Nordhausen can be found at http://www.nizkor.org/hweb/camps/nordhausen/ Nordhausen.html. Let me simply say that Hitler did not attempt to destroy the Jews for religious reasons, although it is clear that he did not actually support the Judeo-Christian Ethic. "The Ten Commandments have lost their validity. Conscience is a Jewish invention, it is a blemish like circumcision" (47) according to Hitler.

But Hitler and the Nazis did not just wage war against the Jews; they also grappled with the Churches of Germany. The Nazis believed in following Martin Luther's lead in subjecting the Church to the state (48). And on this point Hitler was very clear and never wavered. On March 23, 1933, within a month of taking power, Hitler told the Reichstag that the Church would have to submit itself to Nazi policy (49). In August 1934 Hitler repeated his position in another speech (50).

In July 1935 the Reich Ministry for Church Affairs was created (51) to try to increase the influence of the party over the German Churches. But the Church proved to be difficult to control, and in the end the Nazis lost out during some elections of Church officials in which their choices were rejected. Soon afterwards Nazi attitudes towards the Church started to cool (52).

This change in attitude was expressed by Hitler in a 1937 May Day speech in Berlin; "So long as they concern themselves with their religious problems the State does not concern itself with them. But so soon as they attempt by any means whatsoever—by letters, Encyclica, or otherwise—*to arrogate to themselves rights which belong to the State alone* we shall force them back into their proper spiritual, pastoral activity." (emphasis mine)

From 1937 to 1940, the Nazis slowly distanced themselves from the Churches, and in 1940 threw all German clergy out of the party (53). And by the end of the war, many Christians were in concentration camps, where a number of them died, one of the most famous being Dietrich Bonhoeffer.

Ultimately, the Nazis saw the Church as an organization to be controlled and used like all the other social structures of Germany. And when the Church proved to be an unreliable ally it was ultimately constrained, then persecuted, just as the Jews were, but to a lesser extent because they did not represent the same kind of threat.

And let me add another word of caution here; it is seriously unfair to blame the Church for not doing more to resist. The members of the German Church were Germans, and as such were raised in the same atmosphere as everyone else. Many of them undoubtedly believed the same things Hitler did, but this does not make those ideals "Christian" by proxy. The great thing that Martin Luther did was give us the idea of "solo scriptura," only the Bible determines what is and what is not actual Church doctrine, regardless of what any particular Christian or Jewish believer or denomination practices. All else is foolishness and dishonest to boot.

As the fascist movements fell out of favor with American humanists, they turned to communist-based socialism. And at no time in American history other than the 1960's was this true like it was under Roosevelt. In fact, Roosevelt set the economic and social template that American liberals still follow today. It was Roosevelt who blended fascist economic policy with communist social policy to create modern liberalism.

To begin with, there was nothing "new" about the New Deal (54). Many of FDR's policies came right out of the Italian fascist and Nazi playbooks—and the fascists were more successful at implementing those policies than Roosevelt. Hitler's New Deal was in fact far more successful (55). Let me give you an example of the similarity between the two economies you can research yourself; warplane production.

During the war, both Germany and America looked for a way of maximizing the output of their best aircraft. But unlike Russia, neither America nor Germany owned the means of production—they paid manufacturers to design and build aircraft and other equipment for them. So to get the planes they wanted, both devised a plan whereby secondary companies could be used to manufacture a preferred design, with a small percentage skimmed off to pay the original company for use of that particular design.

The Germans took it a step further, with each manufacturer creating a set of jigs that allowed practically any manufacturing site to build aircraft to the original specifications. This was wildly successful, and it was the reason why in 1944 while American bombers smashed German factories to a pulp aircraft production in Germany actually rose to equal 40% of US aircraft output for that year. In fact, Germany produced more aircraft that year than they had fuel to fly due to extensive damage to their fuel refineries by bomber attacks, or air superiority may have swung back their way making it likely that World War II may have gone on far longer than it did. After all, by the end of the war the Germans were flying jet fighters far superior to anything else around.

Fascist economic policies were in wide use in the United States during the Second World War. By the end of the war, the fascist, government-directed segment of the American economy made up around 45% of the whole U.S.

economic output. But because of Hitler and the misunderstanding of why he killed the Jews, Americans were no longer interested in fascism.

Neither was FDR, though he was fascinated with communism. FDR saw many similarities between his ideas and the communists. Roosevelt thought more highly of the Soviet Union than he did of Great Britain, and told Churchill so (56). Most of FDR's "brain trust" had spent time in the Soviet Union (57).

The most prominent of these was Joseph Davies, whose diplomatic trip to the Soviet Union on behalf of Roosevelt ended up as both a book and movie called "Mission to Moscow" in 1941 and was very influential (58). Roosevelt liberals were actually scornful of traditional Americans (59).

And while it is true that FDR did a great good by America conducting the war, it is also true that he is the one who pursued and insisted on meeting with Stalin (60). Throughout the war, Roosevelt acquiesced to Stalin as much as he could, to the point that Churchill nearly resigned in frustration (61). FDR even went so far as to attempt to lie to the public about Soviet freedom of religion in a press conference held in November 1941. He knew that the American Church was wary of communism and thought it OK to lie if it would help overcome that resistance (62).

When Roosevelt finally got the chance to meet Stalin in Tehran in 1943, private meetings were held in which the two men basically divided up the world between them. FDR went as far as suggesting that the caste system of India should be replaced with a soviet-style government (63). Even today American liberals prefer socialist governments over all others, even governments that are pro-American (64).

Humanism had promised utopia yet delivered death. In the twentieth century between 150 and 180 million people would die for socialism. And when it was over a new dark cloud covered Eastern Europe, and extended its shadow into Western Europe where the vast majority of countries experimented with milder forms of socialism.

But in America, there was finally some resistance to the madness. Some voices began to speak out about the real nature of humanism. And a new battle was about to erupt in a new place.

1. Nietzsche, Friedrich. Beyond Good and Evil. Trans. by R.J. Hollingsdale. Penguin Books, 1973. Page 44.

2. Nietzsche, Friedrich. Beyond Good and Evil. Trans. by R.J. Hollingsdale. Penguin Books, 1973. Page 110.

3. Nietzsche, Friedrich. Beyond Good and Evil. Trans. by R.J. Hollingsdale. Penguin Books, 1973. Page 103.

4. Nietzsche, Friedrich. Beyond Good and Evil. Trans. by R.J. Hollingsdale. Penguin Books, 1973. Page 89.

5. Nietzsche, Friedrich. Beyond Good and Evil. Trans. by R.J. Hollingsdale. Penguin Books, 1973. Page 97.

6. Nietzsche, Friedrich. Beyond Good and Evil. Trans. by R.J. Hollingsdale. Penguin Books, 1973. Page 60.

7. Nietzsche, Friedrich. Beyond Good and Evil. Trans. by R.J. Hollingsdale. Penguin Books, 1973. Page 91.

8. Reitbergen, Peter. Europe: a Cultural History. Routledge, 1998. Page 415.

9. Volkogonov, Dmitri. Lenin: A New Biography. Trans. by Harold Shukman The Free Press, 1994. Page xxxii.

10. Volkogonov, Dmitri. Lenin: A New Biography. Trans. by Harold Shukman The Free Press, 1994. Page 373.

11. Volkogonov, Dmitri. Lenin: A New Biography. Trans. by Harold Shukman The Free Press, 1994. Page 373.

12. Volkogonov, Dmitri. Lenin: A New Biography. Trans. by Harold Shukman The Free Press, 1994. Page 375.

13. Volkogonov, Dmitri. Lenin: A New Biography. Trans. by Harold Shukman The Free Press, 1994. Page 381.

14. Volkogonov, Dmitri. Lenin: A New Biography. Trans. by Harold Shukman The Free Press, 1994. Page 386.

15. Volkogonov, Dmitri. Lenin: A New Biography. Trans. by Harold Shukman The Free Press, 1994. Page 379.

16. Volkogonov, Dmitri. Lenin: A New Biography. Trans. by Harold Shukman The Free Press, 1994. Page 375.

17. Volkogonov, Dmitri. Lenin: A New Biography. Trans. by Harold Shukman The Free Press, 1994. Page 136.

18. Ellis, Edward Robb. Echoes of Distant Thunder. Kodansha International, 1975. Pages 126-127.

19. Ellis, Edward Robb. Echoes of Distant Thunder. Kodansha International, 1975. Page ix.

20. Ellis, Edward Robb. Echoes of Distant Thunder. Kodansha International, 1975. Page 393.

21. Ellis, Edward Robb. Echoes of Distant Thunder. Kodansha International, 1975. Page 427.

22. Ellis, Edward Robb. Echoes of Distant Thunder. Kodansha International, 1975. Page 429.

23. Ellis, Edward Robb. Echoes of Distant Thunder. Kodansha International, 1975. Page 428.

24. Goldberg, Jonah. Liberal Fascism. Doubleday, 2007. Pages 81-82.

25. Goldberg, Jonah. Liberal Fascism. Doubleday, 2007. Page 31.

26. Goldberg, Jonah. Liberal Fascism. Doubleday, 2007. Page 34.

27. Goldberg, Jonah. Liberal Fascism. Doubleday, 2007. Page 31.

28. Goldberg, Jonah. Liberal Fascism. Doubleday, 2007. Page 32.

29. Goldberg, Jonah. Liberal Fascism. Doubleday, 2007. Page 40.

30. Goldberg, Jonah. Liberal Fascism. Doubleday, 2007. Page 14.

31. Goldberg, Jonah. Liberal Fascism. Doubleday, 2007. Page 86.

32. Goldberg, Jonah. Liberal Fascism. Doubleday, 2007. Page 96.

33. Goldberg, Jonah. Liberal Fascism. Doubleday, 2007. Page 107.

34. Goldberg, Jonah. Liberal Fascism. Doubleday, 2007. Page 114.

35. Himmelfarb, Gertrude. One Nation, Two Cultures. Alfred A. Knopf, 1999. Page 53.

36. Himmelfarb, Gertrude. One Nation, Two Cultures. Alfred A. Knopf, 1999. Pages 33-34.

37. Weitz, Eric D. Genocide: Utopias of Race and Nation. Princeton University Press, 2003. Page 55.

38. Steigman, Richard. Holy Reich: Nazi Conceptions of Christianity. Cambridge University Press, 2003. Page 46.

39. Goldberg, Jonah. Liberal Fascism. Doubleday, 2007. Page 88.

40. Goldberg, Jonah. Liberal Fascism. Doubleday, 2007. Pages 111-112.

41. Pera, Marcello, and Joseph Ratzinger (Pope Benedict XVI). Trans. by Michael F. Moore. Without Roots: The West, Relativism, Christianity, Islam. Basic Books, 2006. Page 38.

42. Anderson, Dr. C. Thomas and Don Evevoldsen. Me My Country My God. Winword Publishing. Page 46.

43. Goldberg, Jonah. Liberal Fascism. Doubleday, 2007. Page 9.

44. Goldberg, Jonah. Liberal Fascism. Doubleday, 2007. Page 27.

45. Goldberg, Jonah. Liberal Fascism. Doubleday, 2007. Page 27.

46 Goldberg, Jonah. Liberal Fascism. Doubleday, 2007. Page 28.

47. Rauschning, Hermann. Hitler Speaks. Thornton Butterworth Ltd., 1939. Page 20.

48. Steigman, Richard. Holy Reich: Nazi Conceptions of Christianity. Cambridge University Press, 2003. Page 69.

49. Steigman, Richard. Holy Reich: Nazi Conceptions of Christianity. Cambridge University Press, 2003. Page 116.

50. Steigman, Richard. Holy Reich: Nazi Conceptions of Christianity. Cambridge University Press, 2003. Page 118.

51. Steigman, Richard. Holy Reich: Nazi Conceptions of Christianity. Cambridge University Press, 2003. Page 177.

52. Steigman, Richard. Holy Reich: Nazi Conceptions of Christianity. Cambridge University Press, 2003. Pages 216-218.

53. Steigman, Richard. Holy Reich: Nazi Conceptions of Christianity. Cambridge University Press, 2003. Pages 223-224.

54. Goldberg, Jonah. Liberal Fascism. Doubleday, 2007. Pages 10-11.

55. Goldberg, Jonah. Liberal Fascism. Doubleday, 2007. Pages 146-147.

56. Nisbet, Robert. Roosevelt and Stalin: The Failed Courtship. Regnery Gateway, 1988. Page 97.

57. Goldberg, Jonah. Liberal Fascism. Doubleday, 2007. Page 102.

58. Nisbet, Robert. Roosevelt and Stalin: The Failed Courtship. Regnery Gateway, 1988. Page 16.

59. Kent, Phil. The Dark Side of Liberalism. Harbor House, 2003. Page 115.

60. Nisbet, Robert. Roosevelt and Stalin: The Failed Courtship. Regnery Gateway, 1988. Pages 39-40.

61. Nisbet, Robert. Roosevelt and Stalin: The Failed
Courtship. Regnery Gateway, 1988. Page 66.

62. Nisbet, Robert. Roosevelt and Stalin: The Failed
Courtship. Regnery Gateway, 1988. Page 25.

63. Nisbet, Robert. Roosevelt and Stalin: The Failed
Courtship. Regnery Gateway, 1988. Pages 45-49.

64. Nisbet, Robert. Roosevelt and Stalin: The Failed
Courtship. Regnery Gateway, 1988. Page 110.

Chapter Six
The Battle for America

"How many of these damn things are we going to find?"
-American soldier in Germany entering one of the
concentration camps.

The U.S. Third Army had seen a lot of fighting during the War. This was Patton's army, the one that had blunted the German counterattack the previous winter during the Battle of the Bulge. The one that would end up in Czechoslovakia, further east than any other U.S. force would get.

But nothing could prepare them for what they would find in April 1945. On the 4th of the month Third Army soldiers would stumble onto the first death camp to be liberated by the West at Ohrdruf. There, they found rows of ditches filled with human bodies. Arms literally poked out of the ground in places.

Ohrdruf was part of the Buchenwald
system, which American soldiers entered a week
later on April 11th. The Germans hadn't even
turned the furnaces off when they abandoned it.
On April 29th, the U.S. seventh army entered
Dachau. They found thirty railroad boxcars full
of bodies there.

The American soldiers were stunned.
None of them could grasp the depth of what they
were seeing. Ignorant Holocaust deniers would
like you to believe that a handful of camps, even
large ones, could not kill the millions of people
claimed. They are right. What they are not
telling you, or are too stupid to know is that there
were not a handful of camps. The Buchenwald
concentration camp system included a total of
175 separate locations. There were
approximately 450 or more such individual
camps inside Germany's borders alone.

But to the American soldiers pouring
across the German landscape, those concentration
camps were a watershed. The troops that

liberated them would go home different than they came. Those American soldiers and the story of the camps they liberated would change the course of history in America.

It looked as humanists would win in the 1930s. In 1935, socialist newspapers in the U.S. were proclaiming the birth of a new "Soviet America" (1). U.S. ambassador Joseph Kennedy did not think democracy could continue and thought Great Britain would have to develop a fascist form of government (2). H.G. Wells proclaimed his belief in "Militant Progressivism", telling the Young Liberals at Oxford they needed to become "liberal fascists" and "enlightened Nazis" in 1932 (3).

But there were now other voices, insistent that the madness be resisted. The most important figure was Winston Churchill. Somewhere along the way, Churchill began to see the danger posed by humanist ideology and began to cry out against fascism. Thanks to his stalwart leadership, Great Britain resisted the Nazi onslaught and gave the world some breathing room, as well as the chance to see the concentration camps.

Resistance to humanism first began at the end of World War I. Humanist ideas of utopia crumbled before the bloody assault of reality. For a moment in the 1920s, the humanist movement lost its direction. Books such as *The Sun Also Rises* by Hemingway reflected that disappointment and aimlessness many felt. More importantly, a counter-story began to surface. Those who proposed it claimed that the humanist utopia was a mirage; that moral society was better than a structured society after all.

In 1924, *The MagicMountain* by Thomas Mann documented the failures of humanism to live up to its promises (4). Two years later, the movie *Metropolis* by Fritz Lang would visualize the nightmare of humanism. And even as fascism rose from the ashes of supernationalism, another great voice spoke out against the evil. In the same year that H.G. Wells was pushing fascism, Reinhold Niebuhr was releasing *Moral Man and Immoral Society.*

Niebuhr challenged the idea of the perfectibility of man, one of the central ideas of humanism (5). In 1935, he followed up with the book *The Church Against the World*, in which he criticized the adoption of nationalism and humanism in Western thought (6). For the first time, there was a real counterweight in Western society to humanist totalitarianism.

What the American soldiers saw in the German camps reinforced this bold new voice. Those soldiers stared into the abyss of humanism and chose to reject it. American progressivism was broken against the rocks of the German camps, and would remain so for years afterwards. The resistance that started at the end of World War I would finally coalesce into a movement. The battle for the heart of America was on.

For the rest of the decade and through most of the 1950s those soldiers reigned in the pro-humanist movement of America. The "Red

Scare" was not about the idea that the Russians were coming; it was about understanding the magnitude of destruction those kinds of movements brought with them, a lesson that has been learned the hard way from China to Afghanistan over the last few decades by those who chose to ignore the evidence.

But the real battle for the soul of America did not begin until the Presidential campaign of 1960. Over the preceding decades, humanists had perfected the practice of propaganda in other countries. Such practices had been common in America ever since the days of "yellow journalism" at the end of the 19th century.

Propaganda quickly became standard practice for humanists worldwide. In Russia, where the state ran the schools, communism was a part of the required curriculum. According to Dmitri Volkogonov, "The intellectual diet of Leninism was as compulsory for every Soviet citizen as the Koran is for an observing Muslim" (7). Like all such totalitarian states, the role of art itself was used to reflect the Marxist world view (8), and humanists worldwide still stick to this doctrine, clearly seen in almost all American "art" that is non-traditional.

Lenin wanted the death penalty for free speech, which was written into the Soviet constitution under Article 58. During the communist era, millions would be persecuted and die under this law (9). But the Soviets were not the only practitioners of propaganda and suppression of dissent.

During World War I, Wilson created the Committee on Public Information (notice the socialist-style naming of the department) to "spread the word" about America's involvement in the war. Thousands of "agents" spread out across the country to deliver propaganda to the American people. In all, over 7.5 million public addresses were given by the CPI (10).

Of course when it came to propaganda no one was better than the Nazis. They had a full-time department of Propaganda, Hitler was an incredible public speaker, and German radio was used constantly to promote Nazi ideology. The Nazis made anti-Jewish films (11), and *Triumph of the Will* by Leni Riefenstahl is considered one of the all-time great propaganda films. The film was so important that it was worked over by other important directors to create counter-propaganda. There is a good outline of this on Wikipedia.

America was more difficult to propagandize than Russia or Germany. There was no state control of many cultural institutions in America, and unlike Germany the population was not homogenous. Furthermore, the expanse of America made it difficult to organize propaganda on the level that could reach across enough social strata to be effective.

What humanists in America needed was a medium that would allow it to be more present with its message. Unfortunately for the rest of the world, a technology was coming available which would do exactly that; television.

American liberalism was literally saved and restored to dominance by TV and radio. Now, through entertainment, humanists could advocate their message to the whole country—and eventually the whole world. American liberals took the lessons about propaganda from their forebears, Hitler, Wilson, Mussolini, and FDR (12), and applied them to the new American media.

Liberals began a "culture war" in which they fought to monopolize the media and use that monopoly to influence how other Americans thought and to recruit people to their beliefs. Liberalism began to develop a separate culture, with its own books, movies, language and styles. Mass culture quickly became one of the central tenets of liberalism in the West (13). Over time, socialist ideals became an entrenched part of American society whose birth stretched all the way back to the New Deal (14).

Libreals were helped by the adoption of a new mantra, which basically amounted to "freedom through tyranny". Margaret Sanger had originally promoted the idea of "freedom through socialism" to help advocate for birth control (15). Unlike Europe, libertarianism was a strong force in American politics, and liberals adjusted the tone of their propaganda to appeal to libertarian sentiments. Liberals put forth the idea that if the state could "level the playing field" between people then everyone would somehow be *more* free to pursue their own interests—literally freedom through tyranny.

Nevertheless, little had changed about the nature of the humanist movement. Humanism was a violent movement from the moment of its conception during the French Revolution, and it was no different during the 1960s. One of the central theses of the humanist movements was the need to overthrow "traditional" society and replace it with a "new society". This was not just true among the fascists; it was even truer among the communists.

There is one principle that all of the humanist movements have always agreed on, that the state should have the power to do whatever it wants as long as it has adequate reason for doing so (16). For humanists, "…morals should be defined and practiced on the basis of society's purposes, and everything is deemed moral that helps usher in the final state of happiness" (17).

This was explicitly practiced by not just the fascists, but by the communists as well. "…Lenin and his predecessors assumed that in the name of the happiness of future generations, everything was permitted and moral: the export of revolution, civil war, unbridled violence, social experimentation" (18). During the 1960s these practices would come to China on a massive scale and to America on a smaller scale. This is what helped make the American radicals of the 60s "…the third great fascist movement of the 20th century" (19).

Thus while millions were starved and tortured in China, crime rates in America exploded in the 60s and 70s (20). Leftist students of the 60s were dangerously violent, (21) and I can attest to that personally.

During the 70s I was in grade school and in high school, and I lived in the country, so I regularly rode the bus to school. There were some older students who rode the bus as well, and I was beaten up on the bus ride home on many occasions. This also happened to other students who rode the bus home.

It was not until later that I realized that the violent students during my school years were also the most liberal. They were influenced directly by the ideals of the 60s. Now I am 45 years old, and can honestly say that among the people I know who have criminal records-and I know a fair number-none of them have ever been a conservative. Liberalism still breeds violence just as it always has only now the video ends up on YouTube.

While the 1960s and 70s were a time of liberal ascendancy in America, the 80s and 90s were not. Americans grew tired of the violence and the vitriol of the American left and elected Ronald Reagan in 1980. President Jimmy Carter was an abysmal failure as President, and the economy was slowly being wrecked by socialism. Libertarians decided that if they could be free through the state, they could be even freer without the state. The 1980 election proved to be another turning point in history, and the consequences would be more far-reaching than anyone ever expected.

What liberals do not get is that the Reagan Presidency and the Republican ascendancy were about more than angry white guys. Politically, Reagan checked the power of liberalism to spread legally and culturally. And economically, Reagan began to undo the damage done by liberalism.

In the 90s, the conservative movement nearly finished off liberalism. The balanced budgets and limiting of government spending and influence further fueled the prosperity from the

1980s. And something amazing happened—the crime rate actually went down significantly (22). Conservative ascendancy seemed to have the answer to humanism. But it was all about to fall apart again. Literally this time.

1. Susman, Warren. Culture as History. Pantheon Books, 1973. Page 80.

2. Robinson, Derek. Invasion 1940. Carroll & Graf Publishers, 2005. Page 41.

3. Goldberg, Jonah. Liberal Fascism. Doubleday, 2007. Page 21.

4. Reitbergen, Peter. Europe: a Cultural History. Routledge, 1998. Page 418.

5. Moseley, James G. A Cultural History of Religion in America. Greenwood Press, 1981. Page 107.

6. Moseley, James G. A Cultural History of Religion in America. Greenwood Press, 1981. Page 117.

7. Volkogonov, Dmitri. Lenin: A New Biography. Trans. by Harold Shukman The Free Press, 1994. Page xxx.

8. Volkogonov, Dmitri. Lenin: A New Biography. Trans. by Harold Shukman The Free Press, 1994. Page 77.

9. Volkogonov, Dmitri. Lenin: A New Biography. Trans. by Harold Shukman The Free Press, 1994. Pages xxxvii - xxxviii.

10. Goldberg, Jonah. Liberal Fascism. Doubleday, 2007. Page 110.

11. Sadar, Ziauddin, and Merryl Wyn Davies. Why Do People Hate America? Disinformation Co. Ltd., 2002. Pages 45-46.

12. Goldberg, Jonah. Liberal Fascism. Doubleday, 2007. Page 302.

13. Reitbergen, Peter. Europe: a Cultural History. Routledge, 1998. Page 445.

14. Nisbet, Robert. Roosevelt and Stalin: The Failed Courtship. Regnery Gateway, 1988. Pages 108-109.

15. Goldberg, Jonah. Liberal Fascism. Doubleday, 2007. Page 273.

16. Goldberg, Jonah. Liberal Fascism. Doubleday, 2007. Page 131.

17. Pera, Marcello, and Joseph Ratzinger (Pope Benedict XVI). Trans. by Michael F. Moore. Without Roots: The West, Relativism, Christianity, Islam. Basic Books, 2006. Page 73.

18. Volkogonov, Dmitri. Lenin: A New Biography. Trans. by Harold Shukman The Free Press, 1994. Page xxxi.

19. Goldberg, Jonah. Liberal Fascism. Doubleday, 2007. Page 165.

20. Himmelfarb, Gertrude. One Nation, Two Cultures. Alfred A. Knopf, 1999. Page 24.

21. Goldberg, Jonah. Liberal Fascism. Doubleday, 2007. Pages 171-188.

22. Himmelfarb, Gertrude. One Nation, Two Cultures. Alfred A. Knopf, 1999. Page 21.

Chapter Seven
Resurrection

"...we have to be strong because in this world only force is
respected."
-Bosnian President Alija Izetbegović during the Goražde
crisis.

I have only seen a concentration camp
one time, on TV in the early 1990s. It was at the
height of the Bosnian conflict, and Nightline was
playing some footage shot from a moving vehicle
that showed Muslim men lining the road behind
barbed wire. It is one of those images I will
never forget. I can close my eyes and still see the
ragged men lining the barbed-wire fence along
the road.

Of course the Serbian camps such as
those at Omarska and Trnopolje were small
potatoes compared to their forbears in places like
Auschwitz and Treblinka. But they are an
important marker on the road of our descent.

They are a revelation which we must be able to read properly if we are to survive as people of faith.

The modern liberal establishment has worked hard to portray people of faith as vicious and violent, and humanists as innocent and pure. So the first lesson we must take from Bosnia and Kosovo is that despite all the P.R., nothing has changed. Humanism is still as violent and deadly as it ever was. But now, it is learning to hate a new group of people; Muslims.

Almost from the moment of the breakup of Yugoslavia the persecution began. Milosević took power in 1989 by working the Serbian crowds into frenzies over Kosovo (1). He vowed Kosovo would remain in Serbian hands forever (2). That same year, the Serb military occupied Kosovo under Milosević's orders.

The Serbs began persecuting the Muslims almost immediately (3). Muslims under Serbian rule would be forced to wear white armbands and were thought of by the Serbs the same way the

Germans thought of the Jews (4). It was
happening all over again, only this time it would
happen in front of the whole world.

The Serbian government at the time was a
combination of communism and nationalism—in
other words, fascist. Milosević painted the
Serbian state as the last bastion of communist
ideals (5). He was the penultimate strong fascist
leader of our time. And his ideology was
frighteningly familiar.

Once it was clear that Yugoslavia would
break apart, Milosević's goal was to create a
"greater Serbia" encompassing as much territory
as possible (6). Just as Hitler did before him,
Milosević wanted to create a "racially pure" state
(7). The Bosnian state was called a "Muslim
Bastard" that was squatting on Serbian land—
never mind the fact that they had been there for
centuries (8). The Muslims were seen merely as
an obstacle to be removed (9)

Strangely enough, open fighting began
over Croatia's declaration of independence. But

the Croats were much tougher than expected, and Germany came down on the side of their former ally to which they still had close ties (10). In 1995, a Croatian counteroffensive ended the war with Serbia. The Bosnian Muslims would not be so lucky—when it was their turn, no one would speak out on their behalf. So while Croatian independence was secured through being an integral part of the European community, Bosnian independence was denied for the exact same reason.

Bosnians were unfortunate enough to be caught between the Croats and Serbs both politically and geographically. Both Croatians and Serbians accused the Muslims in Bosnia of scheming to create a Muslim state (11). It wasn't just the Serbs making the accusations; Croatian President Franjo Tudjman added his voice to the chorus (12). In fact, both the Croatians and Serbians were racially motivated. The only difference was that the Serbs were in general more active.

The serious atrocities took place when the Serbs fell on hapless Bosnia. The Serbs were confident the West would not intervene when the war began in 1991 (13). Milosević himself knew the West would not defend Bosnia (14). The war began almost the moment Bosnia declared independence in 1992, when the Bosnian Serbs responded by walking out and forming their own government (15).

By April 1992, the Serbs were beginning the process of driving the Muslims out of Bosnia (16). They created a reign of terror that included the concentration camps I saw that night on TV (17). Eventually half of all Bosnians would be forced from their homes (18). While the vast majority of perpetrators of ethnic cleansing were Serbs (19), this was not always the case. In 1993, Croats slaughtered over 100 Muslims at Ahimici, including women, children, and the elderly (20).

Much of what we hear in the public domain from government officials is little more than propaganda. But there are occasions, such as Hitler's claim of disdain for Jews because he thought them communist, that gives that next level of clarity to a position or philosophy. And the Serbs would make just such a statement during the battle over the eastern city of Goražde, when they described the city as "…the landlink through which Muslims would *push an Islamic arrowhead into the heart of Europe*" (emphasis mine) (21).

Thus, in a single sentence the Serbians revealed the truth about the nature of the war in Bosnia. It was not a religious war; it was a *war against religion, the Muslim religion.* Hitler saw the Jews not just as an "inferior" race, but as a danger to Germany and the world, claiming that the Jews were using the media and international finance to rule the world. Less than a hundred years later, the Serbs would use the same reasoning to wipe out the Muslims; *they stole out land and oppressed our people and must be destroyed so we can be safe.* And if the response of the other European nations was any indication, they seemed perfectly willing to allow the Serbs to do their dirty work for them.

U.N. officials intentionally downplayed Serbian atrocities (22). Britain refused to blame the Serbs for their actions, simply wanting to allow the conflict to end on its own (23). The British and French threatened to withdraw the paltry forces they had in Bosnia if the U.S. pressed for a lifting of the arms embargo and the bombing of Serbian military targets (24). U.N. troops even allowed the Serbs to walk off with 18 anti-aircraft guns (25). Canadian General Lewis MacKenzie went so far as to accuse the Bosnians of killing their own people (26). Russia was a solid supporter of the Serbs the entire time and still is today.

In the U.S., the demand for action built quickly. Elie Weisel took Clinton to task over Bosnia at the dedication of the Holocaust Memorial (27). Madeleine Albright confronted Colin Powell about the need to intervene (28). America led the way in trying to end the war with the Vance-Owens plan but had to abandon it due to resistance from the Europeans (29).

It was the fall of Srebrenica in 1995 that marked the turning point in the war. On the one hand, Srebrenica was the largest single act of genocide in Europe since the Nazis (30). But the picture of a Bosnian Muslim woman who hung herself out of despair named Ferida Osmanovic changed the public perception of the war in the U.S. Al Gore began to push for action after his daughter saw the picture on the front page of the newspaper and started questioning why more was not being done. Pushing for intervention in Bosnia was the best thing Al Gore has ever done, far better than all his work on "global warming" put together.

Reluctantly, the other NATO powers were forced to agree to allow airstrikes in a limited capacity. But it was enough to end the bloodshed the next year. And when Serbia decided to crack down on Kosovo in 1998, America and the Kosovars were better prepared.

The Albanians had already put in place a supply network to provide weapons, and it did not take very long for a second round of NATO airstrikes to end the conflict the following year with only minor casualties.

But the ugly truth is that Bosnia was the result of international, especially European, ideology (31). The conflict was one of several that had the aim of crushing resistance to the international order—especially, in the case of Bosnia, perceived Muslim resistance (32). Eric Weitz points out, "The U.S. Government and others had intelligence reports on the atrocities being committed but tried to keep the information under wraps…" (33).

A more succinct view was expressed by French sociologist Jean Baudrillard in *Libération*; "What the West wants to impose on the world, from here on out and in the guise of universals, are not completely disjointed values, but it's lack of values" (34). What no one knew at the time was that these efforts were also being pursued in

America. And much as in Bosnia, innocents would die in order to enforce the New World Order. Only this time it would involve an act of treason against the American people.

1. Silber, Laura and Allan Little. Yugoslavia: Death of a Nation. Penguin Books, 1995. Page 58.

2. Silber, Laura and Allan Little. Yugoslavia: Death of a Nation. Penguin Books, 1995. Page 63.

3. Mills, Nicholas and Kira Brunner, Editors. The New Killing Fields. Basic Books, 2002. Page 91.

4. Weitz, Eric D. Genocide: Utopias of Race and Nation. Princeton University Press, 2003. Pages 204-205.

5. Weitz, Eric D. Genocide: Utopias of Race and Nation. Princeton University Press, 2003. Page 191.

6. Silber, Laura and Allan Little. Yugoslavia: Death of a Nation. Penguin Books, 1995. Page 26.

7. Weitz, Eric D. Genocide: Utopias of Race and Nation. Princeton University Press, 2003. Page 190.

8. Weitz, Eric D. Genocide: Utopias of Race and Nation. Princeton University Press, 2003. Page 220.

9. Mahmutćehojić, Rusmir. The Denial of Bosnia. Pennsylvania State University Press, 2000. Page 29.

10. Silber, Laura and Allan Little. Yugoslavia: Death of a Nation. Penguin Books, 1995. Pages 197-200.

11. Silber, Laura and Allan Little. Yugoslavia: Death of a Nation. Penguin Books, 1995. Page 210.

12. Mahmutćehojić, Rusmir. The Denial of Bosnia. Pennsylvania State University Press, 2000. Page 46.

13. Silber, Laura and Allan Little. Yugoslavia: Death of a Nation. Penguin Books, 1995. Pages 126-127.

14. Silber, Laura and Allan Little. Yugoslavia: Death of a Nation. Penguin Books, 1995. Page 219.

15. Silber, Laura and Allan Little. Yugoslavia: Death of a Nation. Penguin Books, 1995. Pages 215-216.

16. Silber, Laura and Allan Little. Yugoslavia: Death of a Nation. Penguin Books, 1995. Page 222.

17. Silber, Laura and Allan Little. Yugoslavia: Death of a Nation. Penguin Books, 1995. Pages 244-250.

18. Silber, Laura and Allan Little. Yugoslavia: Death of a Nation. Penguin Books, 1995. Page 252.

19. Cushman, Thomas, and Stjepan G. Meštrović, Editors. This Time We Knew. New York University Press, 1996. Page 46.

20. Silber, Laura and Allan Little. Yugoslavia: Death of a Nation. Penguin Books, 1995. Page 296.

21. Silber, Laura and Allan Little. Yugoslavia: Death of a Nation. Penguin Books, 1995. Page 325.

22. Cushman, Thomas, and Stjepan G. Meštrović, Editors. This Time We Knew. New York University Press, 1996. Pages 48-52.

23. Cushman, Thomas, and Stjepan G. Meštrović, Editors. This Time We Knew. New York University Press, 1996. Pages 70-71.

24. Silber, Laura and Allan Little. Yugoslavia: Death of a Nation. Penguin Books, 1995. Page 334.

25. Silber, Laura and Allan Little. Yugoslavia: Death of a Nation. Penguin Books, 1995. Page 332.

26. Silber, Laura and Allan Little. Yugoslavia: Death of a
Nation. Penguin Books, 1995. Page 310.

27. Mills, Nicholas and Kira Brunner, Editors. The New
Killing Fields. Basic Books, 2002. Page 3.

28. Mills, Nicholas and Kira Brunner, Editors. The New
Killing Fields. Basic Books, 2002. Page 75.

29. Silber, Laura and Allan Little. Yugoslavia: Death of a
Nation. Penguin Books, 1995. Pages 287-288.

30. Silber, Laura and Allan Little. Yugoslavia: Death of a
Nation. Penguin Books, 1995. Page 350.

31. Cushman, Thomas, and Stjepan G. Meštrović, Editors.
This Time We Knew. New York University Press, 1996.
Page 83.

32. Cushman, Thomas, and Stjepan G. Meštrović, Editors.
This Time We Knew. New York University Press, 1996.
Page 85.

33. Weitz, Eric D. Genocide: Utopias of Race and Nation.
Princeton University Press, 2003. Page 216.

34. Baudrillard, Jean. Asserbissement occidental.
Libération, July 3, 1995. Page 4.

Chapter Eight
Betrayal

"…the man has been first; in the future the system must be first."
-Frederick Winslow Taylor, *The Principles of Scientific Management.*

It was the evening of January 30, 1933, and Adolf Hitler stood in a balcony of the Presidential Palace while he listened to the cheering of thousands of his fellow Germans. Joseph Goebbels would later write in his diary that "The German revolution has begun!"

But Hitler was well aware he was still on politically shaky ground. The Nazis had never received a majority of the seats in the Reichstag, and Hitler himself had come up short in two previous attempts at being elected President. Like so many other political decisions in history, Hitler became Chancellor in a backroom deal that didn't involve a single voter.

The Nazis knew they needed some sort of event to solidify public support and consolidate political power. The 1920s and 30s were a time of upheaval in Germany, and the ideas of communism were gaining ground. The Weimar Republic was ridiculously unstable. Today's political success could easily be followed by tomorrow's defeat if Hitler did not consolidate power quickly. Hitler needed to prove to the German people that he needed to remain in power. Unfortunately for the rest of us, Hitler would get the event he was looking for.

On the evening of February 27, less than a month after Hitler took power, Marinus Van Der Lubbe was caught setting fire to the Reichstag building. While the circumstances may never be fully known, it appears as if SA troops assisted Van Der Lubbe during his efforts, and probably contributed to the size of the fire. Hitler needed proof that his enemies were too dangerous to be allowed to continue, and now he had it.

The Nazis took full advantage, fanning the fire by unleashing a barrage of propaganda designed to convince the public that the communists were about to start a civil war. The effects of the propaganda allowed Hitler to get the President, an aged Hindenburg, to sign laws allowing for the prosecuting of the Nazis' political enemies and placing Prussia under Nazi control. New elections had been scheduled for March 5, less than a week away from the date of the fire, and the Nazis were desperate to defeat their enemies.

In those elections the Nazis increased their number of seats by 1/3. It was obvious to the politicians of the Reichstag that momentum had swung solidly in the Nazi's favor. On March 23, the Reichstag passed the Enabling Act that made Hitler dictator. The vote wasn't even close.

People now look at the Reichstag fire and see a staged political event. And that may very well be true. But keep in mind that viewing the events around the Reichstag fire as nothing more than a political machination is missing the point. The real issue was the atmosphere in which it was carried out. The Nazis had spent decades battling the communists in the streets, and at times it really did look like civil war was about to break out. There *was* a small civil war in Austria for a few days in February 1934.

Nazi propaganda fed the German people a steady diet of fear about the communists, a steady stream of propaganda vilifying the all-powerful Jews. The secret to the rise of the Nazis is not that they proved their enemies wrong in civil debate and public policy; instead, they persuaded the German people the Jews and communists were *evil and dangerous*. They did not persuade the people the Jews and communists were incorrect; they persuaded the German people they *needed to be stopped*.

Now let us fast forward to 65 years later, December 20, 1998. President Bill Clinton is in trouble. The Monica Lewinski scandal has struck a nerve with the House of Representatives, which would eventually vote to impeach him. Clinton had been elected President of the United States twice, but both times with a minority of the vote. No President since Richard Nixon had been on such shaky political ground.

But Bill Clinton's problems were bigger than that. He might have been President, but he was the leader of a political movement that seemed to be dying off in front of his very eyes, and there was nothing he could do about it. The conservative congress that was elected on the heels of Clinton's first Presidential election had carried on the conservative agenda which began over a decade earlier when the Reagan Revolution started.

The 18 years following the Reagan Revolution had to have been a nightmare for Democrats. Not only did Reagan's economic plan work, but it worked well, and the economy grew rapidly during the 1980s. Reagan prepared the country to stand up to the communists, but then offered them the opportunity to join with the West in his famous "Tear Down This Wall" speech—and in 1989 they did.

Clinton's Presidency had fared no better. The conservative movement continued in the 1990s unabated. The Congress elected in 1994 eventually delivered on the idea of balancing the budget, which caused the economy to grow even stronger. In New York, Rudy Guiliani oversaw one of the biggest reductions in crime in the history of the United States, if not the world. Dozens of individual states ran budget surpluses.

There was simply no denying that conservative ideals, much of which was based on and supported by the Churches in America, were correct. The American Liberal political argument lay in a worthless heap, and the party was in a shambles. Rush Limbaugh joked that Americans needed to keep a few Democrats around just as an example of what they were. To millions of Americans, liberalism became immaterial to their everyday lives.

Clinton knew that even if he survived his term in office, the political movement he belonged to very well might not. Democrats simply did not have an adequate answer to what was working. What Bill Clinton needed was a Reichstag fire, and he needed a big one. He needed to convince people that conservatives were *evil and dangerous*.

On February 23, 1993 Clinton tried to start his own fire, by sending government agents against the Branch Davidian compound outside Waco. Four federal agents and six resisters died in the ensuing shootout. But that wasn't the worst of it. The ensuing siege lasted 51 days, finally ending April 19th when tanks were sent to punch holes in the building and pump in tear gas. A controversial fire ensued that has caused a great amount of speculation as to the nature of that attack.

What Clinton did not count on was the black eye he would receive in the media. The American public did not think much of the FBI and ATF taking out Churches, even if they did hold some strange views. Many people of faith had been skeptical of the neutrality of the federal government to begin with. Waco made it clear that Clinton might very well be willing to treat everyday citizens one way and the Christians another. Waco was in fact the first major attempt at religious persecution in the United States.

But out of the ashes of Waco came the events that would once again lead to the resurgence of liberalism. Not directly this time, but through other means. It would be a long and winding road which would lead around the world and back to 9/11. But at the time Waco was the low point in the War on Faith.

The first event to occur took place a mere three days after the shootout at Waco when the WTO bombing occurred on February 26th. Clinton vigorously pursued the attackers and their co-conspirators, and all of them have now been captured. And then another event occurred, about which you probably know little about. A conversation took place that would eventually have a major impact on American politics.

Bill Clinton fired the head of the FBI, William Sessions, on July 20th over Waco. A few days earlier, President Clinton had met with the man who would become FBI Director, Louis Freeh, for an interview. During that conversation President Clinton asked Freeh what he would have done at Waco some three months earlier.

According to Freeh, "…I told the president, my decision would have been to wait" (1). Freeh went on to explain that the aggressive nature of the confrontation is what turned public opinion against the administration, and that the FBI needed some sold justification before moving against the compound (2). Clinton, being the consummate politician, would take that advice to heart. From here on out, he would play defense, and let his enemies have the field. He could not create the event that would galvanize public opinion, but he could encourage America's enemies by feigning weakness.

After the "failed" bombing of the WTO, several of the terrorists involved fled the country, including the most important one, a fellow who called himself Ramzi Yousef. He is going to be at the center of our story, because he is the person who first started planning 9/11.

Yousef ended up in the Philippines, where he began working on another project; a bomb small enough to be easily smuggled onto an airplane without being detected. The campaign was called by a Serbian word, "Bojinka". And here is the important part you need to know; *it was designed to ignite the center fuel tank on a 747 airliner.*

The plan was to place several of the bombs onboard airliners heading across the Pacific, all timed to go off simultaneously. It would have been a devastating attack.

It did not take long for Yousef to perfect his device, which he tried out in the Greenbelt Theatre in Manilla on December 1, 1994 (3). The bomb was a success, and Yousef threw his energy in preparing to use his new device. On December 11, just a few days after the first test, Yousef himself placed one on Philippine Airlines flight 434. Fortunately, he placed the bomb in the wrong location and missed the fuel tank (4).

On January 6, 1995 Yousef and his co-conspirator Abdul Hakim Murad accidentally exploded some chemicals while mixing a bomb in the room they were renting, and Murad was captured trying to retrieve a laptop from the scene. As he was questioned, two very revealing clues came out about the nature of the conspiracy.

The first was that Murad claimed he and Yousef had already begun planning for a second operation that would involve hijacking aircraft. The other was that Murad was already a trained pilot, and others were undergoing pilot training as well (5). When he was eventually caught, Yousef's uncle, Khalid Sheikh Mohammad also verified that the terrorists were planning the use of planes as weapons in 1995 (6).

Yousef was caught in Pakistan not long after, and the two men were brought to America to face justice for their crimes. Nevertheless, the conspirators were still trying to get the instructions for Yousef's new bomb to other terrorists. He wanted the others to blow up a plane while he was behind bars, because he thought that would lead the judge to declare a mistrial. Yousef had not considered that this would have been of limited consequence in a trial about the WTO attack in '93.

Yousef made another mistake by coming to trust a mafia informant who was in the jail cell between the terrorists. Yousef passed enough information along that by May 1996 federal agents knew how the bombs were built and what to look for (7). That is why you have to take your shoes off when going through security to board a plane, and why you are so limited in not being able to take liquids on. The screeners know exactly what they are looking for and have since at least 1996. Yet airport security in America remained lax until after 9/11.

So on the evening of July 17, 1996, flight 800 was blown out of the air, just like Ramzi Yousef planned. But the administration wanted to keep Yousef behind bars; he was a real danger, and deprived the Al Qaeda of one of their most talented bomb makers. Besides that, Yousef was supplying information the United States had no other way to get. So the Clinton administration did what any liberal would do—they covered up the truth.

The FBI aggressively limited NTSB access to information about flight 800 (8). Eventually, John O'Neill ordered the investigation to be cancelled, (9) but that order originally came from the highest levels of the Clinton administration (10). Louis Freeh was apparently not directly involved, and in any case did not have enough evidence or political clout to overrule the President.

Two other influences came into play between 1993 and 1997. The fist was the attempt by the media to smear the victims of Ruby Ridge and Waco. The media used the events to try to tarnish the image of Christians in America (11). And when Timothy McVeigh bombed the Murrah Federal Building in Oklahoma City two years to the day after the end of the standoff at Waco, the media portrayed him as the typical American conservative (12).

The other strand was the installation of George Tenet as head of the CIA in 1997. Now, Clinton appointees were in charge of both of the major federal criminal agencies. Worse, Tenet had absolutely no training for the position; he was a political appointment. George Tenet would later provide the cover Clinton would need to carry out his plans.

The Embassy bombings of August 7, 1998 increased the pressure on Clinton to respond. So Clinton ordered the cruise missile attack on an aspirin factory outside Khartoum,

Sudan. He also gave permission for Bin Laden to be killed in covert operations (13). And he promoted Richard Clarke to the new post of National Coordinator for Security and Counter-terrorism. But Clarke's appointment did nothing but add a layer of bureaucracy (14). Lois Freeh wrote "As titles go, it has a golden ring, but access is what counts in Washington, and Dick Clark had very little" (15).

Nevertheless, by 1998 something was going awry in the Clinton White House. Information was pouring in that Al Qaeda was planning on hijacking aircraft and using them as weapons. It seems that once Clinton grasped the magnitude of the updated Bojinka plot, he began to think of what it would mean if it was carried out. And Bill Clinton made a conscious decision that would change America.

By the time Clinton had to decide whether to pull the trigger and order the attack on Bin Laden that December, he had already made up his mind (16). He waffled behind the advice of

George Tenet, who was worried about the number of casualties, and Clinton concurred (17).

But there were deeper truths in play at the time. Sixteen days before, on December 4, 1998, Clinton received a briefing that strongly verified Al Qaeda plans to attack American targets using hijacked aircraft (18). Killing Bin Laden meant disrupting those preparations, and probably canceling them. And Bill Clinton could not afford to let that happen.

After December 1998 it was a waiting game to see when and where the blow would be struck. In February 1999 Clinton weakened his permission to kill Bin laden, and the CIA did little to follow up (19). The very next month there was another golden opportunity to kill Bin Laden, but once again Tenet stalled and refused to authorize the action according to Sandy Berger (20).

Clinton seemed to expect the attack during his own presidency, and never seriously moved to stop it again. But it didn't occur while

Clinton was in office. Instead, the U.S.S. Cole was targeted in of October 2000. It didn't matter; Al Gore was supposed to be elected in November 2000. If Bojinka did not occur on Clinton's watch, it would occur during Gore's.

But then, one of the most unexpected events in history occurred; George Bush was elected President. Now, 9/11 would happen on *his* watch. Yet President Clinton stuck to his plans, quietly slipping into the background while events continued to unfold.

Bush had no real idea what was coming—he didn't even receive his first full briefing on the hijacking threat until August 6, 2001, just barely more than a month before the attack was launched. It was not the strong warning the new President needed. That report read, "We have not been able to corroborate some of the more sensational threat reporting, such as…Bin Laden wanted to hijack a U.S. aircraft…" (21). This is a strange statement, considering that on July 10, 2001, FBI headquarters was aware of the Phoenix memo calling for some of the Muslims being trained in U.S. flight schools to be monitored (22). And George Tenet, still head of the CIA, was briefed about he case surrounding Zacharias Moussoui in Minnesota on August 23 (23) but said nothing about it in a staff meeting held one week to the day before 9/11 (24).

The security agencies of the United States melted down under the weight of their own inertia, *just as Bill Clinton planned*, leaving the Bush administration holding dust as hundreds of American citizens died. The real story of 9/11 is that of the greatest act of treason ever committed in the history of the United States, by one of its own Presidents, aided and abetted by a sitting director of the CIA, for no other reason than to turn the political tide that was destroying his party.

Nearly 3,000 Americans lost their lives for this vainglorious reason, and 19 men who thought they were dying to bring glory to Allah were sacrificed on its altar as well. They join the ranks of the other 150 plus million people who had died in the previous century simply to feed the preposterous notion that in order for men to be free God must be dead.

1. Freeh, Louis. My FBI. St. Martin's Press, 2005. Page 51.

2. Freeh, Louis. My FBI. St. Martin's Press, 2005. Page 52.

3. Lance, Peter. Cover Up. HarperCollins 2004. Page 39.

4. Lance, Peter. Cover Up. HarperCollins 2004. Pages 40-41.

5. Lance, Peter. Cover Up. HarperCollins 2004. Pages 44-45.

6. The 9/11 Commission Report. W.W. Norton and Company. Page 153.

7. Lance, Peter. Cover Up. HarperCollins 2004. Pages 49-54.

8. Cashill, Jack and James Sanders. First Strike. WND Books, 2003. Page 17.

9. Lance, Peter. Cover Up. HarperCollins 2004. Page 71.

10. Lance, Peter. Cover Up. HarperCollins 2004. Page 6.

11. Cashill, Jack and James Sanders. First Strike. WND Books, 2003. Page 39.

12. Cashill, Jack and James Sanders. First Strike. WND Books, 2003. Page 16.

13. The 9/11 Commission Report. W.W. Norton and Company. Pages 126-127.

14. The 9/11 Commission Report. W.W. Norton and Company. Page 101.

15. Freeh, Louis. My FBI. St. Martin's Press, 2005. Page 297.

16. Patterson, Robert "Buzz". Dereliction of Duty. Regnery Publishing, 2003. Pages 129-130.

17. Minter, Richard. Losing Bin Laden. Regnery Publishing, 2003. Page 200.

18. The 9/11 Commission Report. W.W. Norton and Company. Pages 128-129.

19. The 9/11 Commission Report. W.W. Norton and Company. Page 133.

20. The 9/11 Commission Report. W.W. Norton and Company. Page 140.

21. The 9/11 Commission Report. W.W. Norton and Company. Pages 261-262.

22. The 9/11 Commission Report. W.W. Norton and Company. Page 272.

23. The 9/11 Commission Report. W.W. Norton and Company. Page 275.

24. Lance, Peter. Cover Up. HarperCollins 2004. Page 176.

Chapter Nine
Assault

"We are at war with Islam."
-Sam Harris, *The End of Faith.*

El Dorado, Texas is a quiet little town just
north of U.S. Route 10, on the main road to San
Angelo. But what happened there on the evening
of April 3rd was frighteningly similar to Waco 15
years earlier. Only this time the victims were
Fundamentalist Latter Day Saints, an offshoot of
Mormonism. To their discredit, the Texas
Rangers who took the lead in the raid used the
same kind of jackbooted tactics of their
forebears.

By the end of the evening, over 400
children had been removed from their homes, and
their parents left to struggle with the Texas court
system. If any group of people deserved public
sympathy, it was the FLDS members from the

compound. That should be doubly so as it turned out they were being wrongfully persecuted.

Instead, I happened across the following personal observation on a social networking site, which I wish to keep confidential and not reveal:

"So this, combined with some personal experiences, has led me to believe that fundamentalist Christians, or anyone who takes religion (especially Christianity) too seriously, is psychotic. There should be a national mandate to send all radical, fundamentalist Christians to therapy. They're delusional, and some of them probably need to be on some kind of psychiatric medication. *It is quite ironic that in my encounters, that deeply religious people are really evil, and immoral deep down inside*...once you've removed their outer masks, they are incapable of interacting with the rest of society--except with their own kind of course. They just have a completely skewed perception of the world, and so out of touch with reality. They are so enclosed in their tiny little world, that they are incapable of comprehending anything else.

So far my experiences with non-religious folk have been more positive. More intelligent, self-assured, open-minded, etc.

Maybe fundamentalist religions are for people who are insecure about who they are, so they latch on to this cult for a sense of identity...which is fake in the long run, making them unstable individuals anyway. So all their behavior whether right or wrong is justified as divine or whatnot based on their ludicrous doctrine.

So yes, in conclusion, fundamentalist, radical Christians are lunatics that need to be thrown in mental institutions, so I call for a national intervention on these psychos for the betterment of society. :)"   (Emphasis mine)

I dare not imagine what the smiley face means.

It is these kinds of vicious, hateful, and usually slanderous kinds of attacks that have come to make up the core of the message of American liberalism since 9/11. And events such as the raid on the FLDS compound are meant to be the political equivalent of an 800-pound gorilla throwing itself against the bars of its cage, knowing that sooner or later something will give and it will no longer be constrained.

The truth is the American liberal movement never lost its angry, violent side that developed during the 60s. During the dark years of the 1970s and 1980s liberals focused on consolidating power in those areas where they still held influence, especially the media and school system. The message I shared with you from the internet about the FLDS and the nature of Christianity is the direct result of that strategy.

The struggle between 1980 and 1998 may have been fought underground, but it was vicious nonetheless. While liberals could not always exercise political power, they found hundreds of other ways to exert influence on society, and in many ways the more their power waned, the more vitriolic and destructive they become.

They developed a new kind of warfare, one so insidious that their own parents would have been horrified. When the rebels of the 60s saw the next generation lead the way during the

Reagan Revolution of the 80s, they declared economic war on their own children. Having moved into positions of power in business and education and media over the following two decades, 60s liberals blacklisted their own offspring for being conservatives.

In May 2007, I graduated cum laude from Arizona State University with a bachelor's degree in Journalism. I already had an associate degree in Business Information Systems from Shawnee State University of Ohio, where I also graduated cum laude. I did four years of volunteer work at my Church in the sound and television production departments (two each). I received scholarships for my work during my last two years, and the fall 2006 edition of our online student magazine, of which I was part, won us an award for best independent student magazine in our region from the Society of Professional Journalists.

My college career may have been a resounding success, but the following year was not. I have a special folder in my e-mail account where I store the automated replies and correspondence I have received from job hunting—most online sites send you an e-mail confirming your application was sent. In that folder, I amassed 1,158 pieces of e-mail from online job hunting between March 3 of 2007 and my birthday on July 2, 2008.

During those 16 months I had over a dozen personal interviews and several more preliminary interviews by phone. Yet as I write this, I work as a customer service rep for computer peripherals making $11.50 an hour. Why? Because I am a conservative, and no one wants me around. This is my second book to go along with a completed movie script, and I can't even get a job as a writer.

And I am one of the lucky ones. Last winter, my car broke down and I had to ride the bus to work until I was able to replace it. While riding on the bus one morning I was struck at how many of the other passengers were not college or high school students. They were people my age that never even had the opportunity to rise to my lowly position. They were permanent economic castoffs of the culture war, victims of their own parent's ideology.

Knowing this we should not be surprised then at the savagery launched at people of faith after 9/11. It was the golden opportunity American liberals desperately needed, and they took full advantage. Muslim extremists thought that American liberals would shirk from their attack, and in that they gravely underestimated humanism. Leftists are every bit as brutal as any thug in history, and they quickly showed their true colors.

Yes, liberals want America to withdraw from Iraq, but only because it the invasion of Iraq proved to be an opportunity to focus their hatred on conservatives in a way that the public would eventually come to support. But that does not mean American liberals are hiding under their beds with the family poodle.

Instead, American liberals used 9/11 to launch an all-out assault on religion. Books and web sites impugning religion sprung up like pox. "Indeed, religion is as much a living spring of violence today as it was at any time in the past" writes Sam Harris (1). Through the words of dozens of liberal books and bloggers, the echo of the voice of Hitler can be heard; *these people are dangerous*, his spirit whispers, *and they must be stopped.*

Harris pulls out all the stops in his books and articles, writing "In fact, it is difficult to imagine a set of beliefs more suggestive of mental illness than those that be at the heart of many of our religious traditions" (2). Harris also bemoans the wasted energy people of faith put into their communities; "Think of all the good things human beings will not be doing this world tomorrow because they believe that their most pressing task is to build another Church or Mosque…" (3).

But his is only one in a chorus of voices condemning faith after 9/11. Christopher Hitchens writes that religion is "As well as a menace to civilization, it has become a threat to human survival" (4). He goes on to claim that "All attempts to reconcile faith with science are consigned to failure and ridicule..." (5).

One of the most vocal detractors is the so-called "scientist" Richard Dawkins. Few are more ferocious in their attacks than he is. "The God of the Old Testament is arguably the most unpleasant character in all fiction..." he claims, (6) calling God "...the monster of the Bible" (7). Dawkins smears everyone with the same broad brush; "The Afghan Taliban and the American Taliban are good examples of what happens when people take their scriptures literally and seriously" (8).

Dawkins makes his position, and the position of thousands of other humanists perfectly clear. "My respect for the Abrahamic religions went up in the smoke and choking dust of September 11th. The last vestige of respect for the taboo disappeared as I watched the "Day of Prayer" in Washington Cathedral, where people of mutually incompatible faiths united in homage to the very force that caused the problem in the first place: religion. It is time for people of intellect, as opposed to people of faith, to stand up and say 'Enough!'" (9).

In reviewing the meaning of the music of Metallica, Peter S. Fosil writes, "What religions claim to be 'righteous' is instead corrupt. What they portray as 'pious' is in fact perverse. What they present in 'truth' is in reality deceit" (10). Fosil speaks for thousands of loyal Metallica fans and millions of other liberals with his pungent analysis of Christianity.

Fosil then offers a critique of the movie *Passion of the Christ*: "The popularity of films like The Passion of the Christ (2003) and the militarism of Christian conservatives are explicable on this model, as well. There's good reason why Mel Gibson's execrable snuff film pays scant attention to the resurrection, to the healing, to the feeding, and forgiving parts of the Jesus story. It's because, despite their protestations to the contrary, religious conservatives (Christian and Islamic, alike) really value death" (11).

This is the twisted and perverted view of Christianity that has taken hold in America, thanks to the new liberal assault on faith. In September 2004 Al Gore compared President Bush to terrorists because of his faith (12). Dawkins agrees with this assessment, writing "For most of my purposes, all three Abrahamic faiths can be treated as indistinguishable" (13).

There are three main points to the humanist argument promoted in the public today. First, humanists claim that morality has nothing to do with religion. Hitchens claims "We believe with certainty that an ethical life can be lived without religion" (14). Dawkins also insists there are no moral differences between believers and non-believers (15).

In fact, humanists try to take the high moral road. Harris claims cultural superiority for humanism by stating "It is time for us to admit that not all cultures are at the same stage of moral development" (16). Dawkins asks, "Do we really need policing-whether by God or each other-in order to stop us from behaving in a selfish and criminal manner?" (17) Hitchens goes even further, claiming "Human decency is not derived from religion. It precedes it" (18).

But what about the untold millions of people who died for humanism during the last century or so? Hitchens makes the incredulous claim that "...humanity began to grow up a little in the closing decades of the eighteenth century and opening decades of the nineteenth" (19). Never mind the Terror that followed the French Revolution or Napoleon or Bismarck or Lenin or Hitler or Stalin or the Cultural Revolution in China. According to Hitchens, once humanism came of age all was well (minus all the dying, of course).

Dawkins certainly works hard to dismiss the history of his forebears. What follows is one of the most frightening and dishonest rewritings of history ever attempted. "What matters is not whether Hitler or Stalin were atheists, but whether atheism systematically *influences* people to do bad things", (20) he states. Dawkins follows this line of reasoning to his own sick conclusion, trying to avoid the idea that Hitler and Stalin did what they did in the name of humanism. Instead Dawkins blows smoke at the reader, claiming "Stalin and Hitler did extremely evil things, in the name of, respectively, dogmatic and doctrinaire Marxism, and an insane and unscientific eugenics theory tinged with sub-Wagnerian ravings" (21). Duh. That's what humanists believed at the time, as we have already seen.

The real problem is the humanist Big Lie of Religion; "Religion has killed more people than all the wars put together". Harris calls religion "...the most prolific source of violence in our history…" (22) It is a bold-faced, flat out lie without an ounce of truth in it. According to historian Will Durant, more people died in the 20ᵗʰ century from the political practices of humanism than in *all* the conflicts from Caesar to Napoleon (23).

But the Big Lie of Religion is only part of the bludgeon used by liberals to assault people of faith, and brings them to their second point; religion does not deserve to have a place in the public square. To the humanists, religion has nothing to offer. "Religion spoke its last intelligible or noble or inspiring words long ago…" (24) Hitchens insists.

Instead, they subtly suggest that religion must become a public issue. "It is time we recognized that belief is not a private matter; it has never been merely private," according to Harris, who then adds one of the most chilling statements imaginable; "These are problems of both cultural and psychological engineering" (25).

Harris then goes on to state that as far as he is concerned we are no longer free to believe whatever we want (26). "We have simply lost the right to our myths, and our mythic identities", (27) he proclaims. And in these there is that voice again, coming to us down through the ages, insistent; *these people are dangerous, and they must be stopped.*

Humanists say they are for the separation of Church and *state*, but what they are really after is the separation of Church and *society* (28). As long as traditional religion is respected, they cannot replace it with the religion of humanism. And as you will see, that is exactly what they are aiming for with their third charge; Darwinism is god.

Hitchens is bold enough to come right out and say it. "Now at last you can be properly humble in the face of your maker, which turns out not to be a 'who' but a process of mutation" (29). Dawkins adds his own thoughts the issue, writing, "As a scientist, I am hostile to fundamentalist religion because it actively debauches the scientific enterprise" (30). And like most fascists, he favors indoctrination; "But perhaps you need to be steeped in natural selection, immersed in it, before you can truly appreciate its power" (31).

But here is the one thing all Muslims must know; those friendly, Bush-is-a-monster, we-must-leave-Iraq-now liberals who pretend to be your friends are not. Even now they are plotting your downfall, and calling for it far more consistently than you will ever see on television or read in the paper. It is true that American liberals focus more on the American Churches because they stand in the way of an immediate humanist takeover of the U.S. But just as it is said Muslim terrorists hold to "First Saturday, then Sunday", American liberals have a saying you will never hear out loud but that they hold dear in their hearts; *"First Sunday, then Friday and Saturday"*.

I am only quoting a few major authors out of an avalanche of anti-religious books to be released since 9/11, but they provide a stark example of the building fury towards Islam. And if you do not heed their words, you will suffer dearly for it *because they are already calling for your destruction*.

In fact, nearly every one of these authors single out Muslims as the main enemy of humanism in the long run. They now assault Islam far more virulently than they do Christianity. "Islam, more than any other religion human beings have devised, has all the makings of a thoroughgoing cult of death", (32) Sam Harris puffs. "What is obvious, however, is that the West must either win the argument or win the war. All else is bondage" (33).

Hitchens makes a similar argument; "As I write these words, and as you read them, people of faith are in their different ways planning your and my destruction, and the destruction of all the hard-won human attainments I have touched upon" (34). Slowly that voice begins to emerge more clearly from the background. *Muslims are dangerous, and they must be stopped.*

Sam Harris openly states that "Islam itself" is the problem (35), stating that "…Islam and Western liberalism remain irreconcilable" (36). Brigitte Gabriel claims, "…the Arab Muslim world, because of its' religion and culture, is a natural threat to the civilized world, particularly Western civilization" (37).

But this is more than political rhetoric; it is the demonization of an entire religion. Islam is characterized as a disease that must be purged from the body of mankind, much the way Hitler characterized the Jews. At secularhumanism.org you can read the following; "To me, all diseases are bad—yet some are more acute, more lethal than others. Likewise all religions may be bad, but in my view Islam is the most harmful as regards its negative effects on the individual and on society in general" (38).

From masada2000.org comes this lovely tidbit; "Through centuries of fanatical conquests (Jihads) and terrorism (when Jihads failed), Islam has metastasized into a modern day world cancer" (39). And at www.flex.com they have this to say; "Islam imposes a threat to the whole world which is far worse than deforestation, nuclear destruction or AIDS. It is an insidious, devilish disease creeping into the veins of the world. Every individual must realise the destructive and evil nature of this religion, for it eats away at the very foundation of humanity..." (40).

These are the same kinds of words Hitler used towards the Jews..."This was pestilence, spiritual pestilence, worse than the Black Death of olden times, and the people was being infected with it!" (41) Just as Judaism was a disease then Islam is a disease now. And just as Hitler blamed the Jews for Europe's woes, modern humanists in Europe blame all their social ills on Muslims. "In Italy, 95% of all rapists are Muslims. Eighty-five percent of all murderers are Muslims. Ah, such a wonderful religion of peace! What does the Pope and the rest of the Vatican Church have to say about this? Nothing!" (42)

Having verbally robbed Muslims of their humanity, they feel free to openly call for a purging. In America "The Muslim community in this nation has lost our trust, lost our respect, lost our understanding and compassion for whatever problems it has" according to Gabriel (43). It is a call for a modern witch hunt, and they make their case in no uncertain terms. "Given the link between belief and action, it is clear that we can no more tolerate a diversity of religious beliefs than a diversity of beliefs about epidemiology and basic hygiene" claims Harris (44).

Gabriel goes as far as to use the same "stab-in-the-back" argument used by Hitler about the Jews; "…we find American Muslims stabbing America in the back right in the heartland…" (45). It is nothing more than fear mongering, just like her claim that thousands of terrorists have crossed into America from Mexico (46).

These statements are meant to unequivocally make the case for the persecution of Muslims. Gabriel believes that Muslims should not be afforded the same types of protections as other groups, (47) while Harris is more direct in his feeling on the subject. "Some propositions are so dangerous that it may even be ethical to kill people for believing them" (48) he states. Stalin could not agree more.

But Harris goes even further than this, laying out the ultimate goal of humanism for all to see. For Harris supports imposing Western culture on Muslims through a dictatorship, (49) laying out the rationale for *launching a nuclear first strike* against Muslim nations should they "get the bomb". "In such a situation, the only thing likely to ensure our survival may be a nuclear first strike of our own" (50).

Dawkins writes, "I do not believe there is an atheist in the world who would bulldoze

Mecca…" (51). But we can be sure that is only window dressing, for his fellow humanists are apparently quite willing to nuke Mecca like a ham sandwich at a convenience store. Because in the end, the goals of humanism have always been the same old dream of *Utopia*, expressed with the words, "We can say it even more simply: we need a world government" (52).

What Dawkins and Harris and their cohorts hide is that the West has been at war with the traditional cultures of the world for decades, a secret war that has gone unrecognized despite the fact it has been fought in public where everyone has seen it. It is the most insidious war ever fought, and it is meant to bring the whole world to heel just as it has the West and China and Russia.

And it is a war the humanists are winning.

1. Harris, Sam. The End of Faith. WW Norton and Co.,
2004. Page 26.

2. Harris, Sam. The End of Faith. WW Norton and Co.,
   2004. Page 72.

3. Harris, Sam. The End of Faith. WW Norton and Co.,
   2004. Page 149.

4. Hitchens, Christopher. God is Not Great. Hachette
   Book Group, 2007. Page 25.

5. Hitchens, Christopher. God is Not Great. Hachette
   Book Group, 2007. Pages 64-65.

6. Dawkins, Richard. The God Delusion. Houghton
   Mifflin, 2006. Page 31.

7. Dawkins, Richard. The God Delusion. Houghton
   Mifflin, 2006. Page 46.

8. Dawkins, Richard. The God Delusion. Houghton
   Mifflin, 2006. Page 288.

9. Dawkins, Richard. Time to Stand Up.
   http://www.ffrf.org/.

10. Fosil, Peter S. William Irwin Editor. Metallica and
Philosophy. Wiley-Blackwell, 2007. Page 74.

11. Fosil, Peter S. William Irwin Editor. Metallica and
Philosophy. Wiley-Blackwell, 2007. Page 81.

12. Gelernter, David. Americanism: The Fourth Great
Western Religion. Doubleday, 2007. Page 207.

13. Dawkins, Richard. The God Delusion. Houghton
    Mifflin, 2006. Page 37.

14. Hitchens, Christopher. God is Not Great. Hachette Book Group, 2007. Page 6.

15. Dawkins, Richard. The God Delusion. Houghton Mifflin, 2006. Pages 222-226.

16. Harris, Sam. The End of Faith. WW Norton and Co., 2004. Page 143.

17. Dawkins, Richard. The God Delusion. Houghton Mifflin, 2006. Page 228.

18. Hitchens, Christopher. God is Not Great. Hachette Book Group, 2007. Page 266.

19. Hitchens, Christopher. God is Not Great. Hachette Book Group, 2007. Page 66.

20. Dawkins, Richard. The God Delusion. Houghton Mifflin, 2006. Page 273.

21. Dawkins, Richard. The God Delusion. Houghton Mifflin, 2006. Page 278.

22. Harris, Sam. The End of Faith. WW Norton and Co., 2004. Page 27.

23. Durant, Will. The Age of Faith. Simon and Schuster, 1950. Page 784.

24. Hitchens, Christopher. God is Not Great. Hachette Book Group, 2007. Page 7.

25. Harris, Sam. The End of Faith. WW Norton and Co., 2004. Page 44.

26. Harris, Sam. The End of Faith. WW Norton and Co., 2004. Page 51.

27. Harris, Sam. The End of Faith. WW Norton and Co., 2004. Page 48.

28. Himmelfarb, Gertrude. One Nation, Two Cultures. Alfred A. Knopf. Page 112.

29. Hitchens, Christopher. God is Not Great. Hachette Book Group, 2007. Page 9.

30. Dawkins, Richard. The God Delusion. Houghton Mifflin, 2006. Page 284.

31. Dawkins, Richard. The God Delusion. Houghton Mifflin, 2006. Page 117.

32. Harris, Sam. The End of Faith. WW Norton and Co., 2004. Page 123.

33. Harris, Sam. The End of Faith. WW Norton and Co., 2004. Page 131.

34. Hitchens, Christopher. God is Not Great. Hachette Book Group, 2007. Page 13.

35. Harris, Sam. The End of Faith. WW Norton and Co., 2004. Page 28-29.

36. Harris, Sam. The End of Faith. WW Norton and Co., 2004. Page 111.

37. Gabriel, Brigitte. Because They Hate. St. Martins' Press. Page 105.

38. Mirza, Syed Kamran. Why Critical Scrutiny of Islam Is an Utmost Necessity. http://www.secularhumanism.org/.

39. http://www.masada2000.org/islam.html.

40. http://www.flex.com/~jai/satyamevajayate/index.html.

41. Hitler, Adolf. Mein Kampf. Chapter 1.2 (Online version).

42. http://www.masada2000.org/islam.html.

43. Gabriel, Brigitte. Because They Hate. St. Martins' Press. Page 206.

44. Harris, Sam. The End of Faith. WW Norton and Co., 2004. Page 46.

45. Gabriel, Brigitte. Because They Hate. St. Martins' Press. Page 206.

46. Gabriel, Brigitte. Because They Hate. St. Martins' Press. Page 132.

47. Gabriel, Brigitte. Because They Hate. St. Martins' Press. Page 216.

48. Harris, Sam. The End of Faith. WW Norton and Co., 2004. Page 53.

49. Harris, Sam. The End of Faith. WW Norton and Co., 2004. Page 151.

50. Harris, Sam. The End of Faith. WW Norton and Co., 2004. Page 129.

51. Dawkins, Richard. The God Delusion. Houghton Mifflin, 2006. Page 249.

52. Harris, Sam. The End of Faith. WW Norton and Co., 2004. Page 151.

Chapter Ten
KULTURKAMPF

"The Berlin Wall came down without a single shot being
fired because people on the other side wanted to be like
us..."
-Howard Dean, *Winning Back America*.

In March 2005, Brian Welch was baptized
in the Jordan River like thousands of pilgrims
before him. But Welch was not just another
pilgrim; he had been the lead guitarist for the
popular metal band Korn. Musicians are the
modern prophets of the humanist movement, and
their followers take their religion very seriously.

Welch was simply trying to survive; he
had been part of a culture in which, because of a
lack of any real moral anchor, it was far too easy
to spiral out of control. This is especially true if
you are a popular rock star that has millions of
dollars at your disposal. By his own admission
Welch was heavily into meth during his time

with Korn. His marriage collapsed and he ended up as a single father of a little girl (1). Welch was watching his life fall apart in front of his eyes.

But Welch's response to his predicament was unacceptable; he came to Jesus and surrendered. To his fans he was the ultimate traitor, leaving the religion of humanism for another faith considered its mortal enemy. The response to his new faith was not pretty. Fellow musician Jonathan Davis responded with "That shit's crazy" to a Sydney newspaper (2). Korn wrote songs about Welch and his treachery. "You're the infection my friend…" the band intoned.

An ex-fan posted a message at www.roadrunnerrecords.com that was even more to the point; "…this motherfucker is insane in his head. Hopefully he will just go away and die" (3). That's how humanists treat turncoat prophets. Despite claims of "tolerance" there is only humanism to those who are its adherents and all else is putrid filth.

Truth be known, humanists would just as soon see Welch die in a pool of his own vomit in a filthy alley than get his life straightened out and raise his daughter if it means his religious conversion. Welch as a human being means nothing to them and never did. He was only valued when he was willing to be their pied piper, and now that he's not he's just another piece of shit that deserves to die.

The only thing that really matters to humanists is culture, because it is through culture that humanism has been able to successfully expand its borders. Welch, by turning his back on that culture threatens its existence by devaluing it, because that is what a culture is; a shared community of thought and action. When a culture begins to bleed adherents it eventually dies off and humanism cannot allow that since it is now a cultural movement before a political one. Thus the reason for the current animus towards Mr. Welch.

It is this focus on culture that separates modern liberals from their socialist forefathers. Not that they are any less socialist, but American liberalism sees "culture" as the antidote to traditional society instead of political totalitarianism. Liberal ideas can be better enforced through culture than government. Whereas old-school humanists wanted to use the state to build society, modern liberals want to use the society to build the state. And they have been frighteningly successful at it.

Like most bad ideas, this one began in communist Russia. Geographically, the Soviet Union covered a multitude of different cultures. The soviets could not wipe the different cultures out, so they decided on a compromise strategy in which they would support the different cultures they ruled over but only as a subset to the overarching Soviet culture (4). It was perfectly acceptable to keep you Armenian culture, as long as you remained a good soviet first.

What the Soviets discovered was that over time, those local cultures formed a bond with the soviet culture, making the soviet culture a part of their own identity. When they realized what they had discovered, the American liberals of the 60s and 70s used the tactic with devastating effectiveness. The liberal movement portrayed itself as the defender the oppressed, and quickly won over groups like the American Indians and Blacks.

Overseas, upstart Catholic Priests invented "liberation theology" to do the same thing in third-world countries. While this may have helped Rome to maintain its relevancy in poorer areas of the world, it also caused Rome for a while to be identified as pro-socialist by conservative Christians in America, widening the gap between the two Churches.

Thus liberals entered into a new kind of warfare designed to ingest other cultures. It is the ultimate form of Kulturkampf. Whereas Mussolini wanted "Everything inside the state, nothing outside the state", American liberals now want "Everything inside the culture, nothing outside the culture". American liberals and their allies consider themselves culturally superior to the rest of the world (5).

The rest of the world, including the American Church has been unforgivably slow to respond. In America today the culture war is mostly over; not only have liberals radically transformed the nation (6), but even most of the Church in America has been absorbed. You know a religion is dying when its leaders preach that freedom is a first principle instead of piety.

With the advent of modern communications, liberalism can now do what Hitler and Stalin could not; enslave the whole world. As technology has spread around the globe, liberalism has ridden on its coattail. It is through the importation of American culture that liberalism is imposing its kingdom of immorality on the rest of the world (7).

This culture has established itself in nearly every city of the globe, especially among the young. The goal is to make other cultures American liberal at heart in order to effect change and control in those countries. As pointed out in *Why Do People Hate America?*, "Thus, American-led globalization uses pop music, television and style products to transform the identity of young people in the developing world into a commodity" (8). It is the electronic version of the Borg—and a dangerous threat to conservative cultures around the world.

What this really amounts to is a form of imperialism based on culture rather than race or nationality. Pope Benedict writes, "…it only goes to follow that seeking to export these same (liberal) institutions to other cultures or traditions that are different from our own would be an act of imperialism" (9).

The American people may see the exportation of American movies and television as a small matter, but entertainment products are now America's *number one* export. Not steel, computers, or grain, but television programs, video games, and movies. And overseas consumers have become attached to American liberal ideals because "…the products of the culture became advertisements of the culture itself" (10).

The left has used the media to invade the Islamic countries of the world in a way that is shocking to those living under the bombardment. America is now a culturalistic empire instead of imperialistic (11), squeezing other cultures out of their own societies like a giant psychic python (12).

Movies and TV, along with music, create American cultural dominance in foreign countries, including the Middle East (13). Liberals run media outlets in the Middle East, such as the left-wing Radio Al Mahaba. And with the advent of satellite dishes, Western TV is everywhere (14). Since the conquest of Iraq, the United States government is creating new radio and television stations to pump out ever larger doses of Western culture into the Muslim world (15). International Planned Parenthood Federation has over 70 local offices in India, handing out condoms and undermining the traditional values of the country (16). Third-world representatives rioted at a U.N. conference on Women held in Beijing when American women tried to force themselves sexually onto the other women (17).

This assault is not accidental or secondary to providing services to poor people; "Imitation is not only the sincerest form of flattery; it is, over the long term, the most reliable way to implement Western values and practices" (18). The author who wrote that also predicts that eventually the whole world will become like Europe (19). For European Muslims this means "...secularization will become stronger and the power of the mosques, the minarets, and the muezzin to underlie their group spirit will inevitably weaken as well" (20).

Many Muslims are aware of the war against faith. Dinesh D'Souza writes that "Radical Islam's most serious charge is that there is a war against Islam being waged by America, the fountainhead of Atheism" (21). Accordingly, "Western pop culture…is viewed by the jihadists as the main weapon in America's psychological war against Islam. Some jihadists fear the cultural offensive of the United States more than they fear its weapons" (22).

Many Muslims are dismayed by the invasion of American culture. "To the other cultures of the world, there is something deeply alien about the absolute secularism that is developing in the West. They are convinced that a world without God has no future" (23). They view the depravity of the West differently than humanists, and that depravity has become a rallying cry for radicals. "The radical Muslims are convinced that America and Europe have become sick, demented societies that destroy religious belief, undermine traditional morality, dissolve the patriarchal family, and corrupt the innocence of children" (24). Muslims look into the abyss of humanism just as those American soldiers did in 1945, and are similarly repulsed. Over 80% of all Muslims want increased moral constraints on society (25).

The problem is only acerbated by the posturing of the American Churches. When pompous blowhards like John Hagee spew forth nonsense such as, "America is now engaged in a bloody battle with religious fanatics on a mission from their god to kill Christians and Jews" (26) he misses the point altogether. Hagee may believe in his feverish mind that they hate us for our freedom, prosperity, and culture (27), but he is dead wrong.

9/11 did not occur because America would not retaliate, as Hagee thinks (28). It occurred because America is decadent and evil, because the Churches have not protected their own values from desecration, much less anyone else's. Muslims see America as a nation that has rejected Christianity for all practical purposes and themselves as the last stronghold of monotheism (29). "Fundamentalists portray America as a nominally Christian but de facto Atheist society" (30), which is a remarkably accurate representation of the situation.

We do not understand Muslims in American Churches because we are no longer truly Christians (31). We have been assimilated by American liberalism, and in reality we place those values of freedom, prosperity, and culture Mr. Hagee alluded to above the values of the Bible. Christians in America are infidels just like everybody else; we are just more civilized about it.

If we were serious, we would handle our own business, and we would not be making an avalanche of smut to export to the rest of the world in the first place. Those "terrorists" who flew those planes on 9/11 saw themselves doing for us what we as Christians would not do for ourselves; fighting back. And yet has the Church shut down Hollywood since 9/11? Of course not. We enjoy "Desperate Housewives" too much. Christians are not like an addict in denial, we *are* an addict in denial, and persuading ourselves it is OK to have another god above Jehovah. Jesus calls us to be believers first, but in reality we are not.

Instead, we make up a large contingent of the troops that have been stationed in Iraq throughout the occupation. We believe in our grandiose visions of bringing our faith to people who do not understand why we cannot stand up to a few sideshow freaks in our own nation. What do we have to offer them? How are we going to go to them and say that they should not stand up for their own families? If we would stand up *here* we wouldn't need to be *there*.

It might make you feel proud to wear a U.S. military uniform, but I have a few ideas that might actually help the situation. And for God's sake, quit being so bellicose when Muslims act to defend their faith. God knows we won't defend ours.

1. Dickerson, John. Korn Free. Phoenix New Times, Volume 39, Number 25. June 19-25, 2008. Page 26.

2. Dickerson, John. Korn Free. Phoenix New Times, Volume 39, Number 25. June 19-25, 2008. Page 28.

3. Dickerson, John. Korn Free. Phoenix New Times, Volume 39, Number 25. June 19-25, 2008. Page 30.

4. Weitz, Eric D. Genocide: Utopias of Race and Nation. Princeton University Press, 2003. Page 60.

5. Gabriel, Brigitte. Because They Hate. St. Martins' Press. Page 185.

6. D'Souza, Dinesh. The Enemy at Home. Doubleday, 2007. Page 20.

7. D'Souza, Dinesh. The Enemy at Home. Doubleday, 2007. Page 21.

8. Saddar, Ziauddin, and Merryl Wyn. Why Do People Hate America? Disinformation Co., LTD. 2002. Page 125.

9. Pera, Marcello, and Joseph Ratzinger (Pope Benedict XVI). Trans. by Michael F. Moore. Without Roots: The West, Relativism, Christianity, Islam. Basic Books, 2006. Page 3.

10. Susman, Warren. Culture as History. Pantheon Books, 1973. Page xxiv.

11. Saddar, Ziauddin, and Merryl Wyn. Why Do People Hate America? Disinformation Co., LTD. 2002. Page 65.

12. Saddar, Ziauddin, and Merryl Wyn. Why Do People Hate America? Disinformation Co., LTD. 2002. Page 104.

13. Saddar, Ziauddin, and Merryl Wyn. Why Do People Hate America? Disinformation Co., LTD. 2002. Page 139.

14. D'Souza, Dinesh. The Enemy at Home. Doubleday, 2007. Page 97.

15. Saddar, Ziauddin, and Merryl Wyn. Why Do People Hate America? Disinformation Co., LTD. 2002. Page 137.

16. www.ippf.org/en/Where/IN.htm.

17. D'Souza, Dinesh. The Enemy at Home. Doubleday, 2007. Page 120.

18. Mandelbaum, Michael. The Case for Goliath. Public Affairs (Perseus), 2005. Page 211.

19. Mandelbaum, Michael. The Case for Goliath. Public Affairs (Perseus), 2005. Page 204.

20. Reitbergen, Peter. Europe: a Cultural History. Routledge, 1998. Page 463.

21. D'Souza, Dinesh. The Enemy at Home. Doubleday, 2007. Page 177.

22. Saddar, Ziauddin, and Merryl Wyn. Why Do People Hate America? Disinformation Co., LTD. 2002. Page 137.

23. Pera, Marcello, and Joseph Ratzinger (Pope Benedict XVI). Trans. by Michael F. Moore. Without Roots: The West, Relativism, Christianity, Islam. Basic Books, 2006. Page 80.

24. D'Souza, Dinesh. The Enemy at Home. Doubleday, 2007. Page 14.

25. Saddar, Ziauddin, and Merryl Wyn. Why Do People Hate America? Disinformation Co., LTD. 2002. Page 28.

26. Hagee, John. Jerusalem Countdown. Front Line, 2006. Page 1.

27. Hagee, John. Jerusalem Countdown. Front Line, 2006. Page 28.

28. Hagee, John. Jerusalem Countdown. Front Line, 2006. Page 13.

29. D'Souza, Dinesh. The Enemy at Home. Doubleday, 2007. Pages 117-118.

30. D'Souza, Dinesh. The Enemy at Home. Doubleday, 2007. Page 115.

31. D'Souza, Dinesh. The Enemy at Home. Doubleday, 2007. Page 86.

Chapter Eleven
Uprising

"The Matrix cannot tell you who you are."
-Trinity, from *The Matrix*.

Now you know the nature of the war on faith. What you may not realize is how close we are to slipping off the tightrope we are walking. In the spring of 2008 the Supreme Court, because of the appointments made by George Bush, decided 5-4 that citizens in America had the right to own a gun.

But George Bush was never supposed to be President. Al Gore was. Gore's appointments were supposed to be deciding 5-4 that it would be constitutional to make believers-all believers, including Muslims-register their copies of their scriptures with the state, imposing restrictions on the number of copies an individual would be allowed to own. We were not supposed to be talking about providing social services through religious programs, but about limiting the size and location of religious meetings. Recently Senator Grassley has demanded the financial records of contributors to several Christian ministries. I know, because my Church was one of those he made the request to. Fortunately, Senator Grassley has no power to collect the names of Christians who contribute to the Church, but he was supposed to under an Al Gore Presidency.

Nevertheless this is only a temporary setback, and the American left is well aware of this. They have a secret weapon that will change the face of America forever; Che Guevara. He lives in the hearts of the 12 million plus illegal aliens that currently reside in the U.S. And very soon they will be given amnesty and made into American citizens.

When they are, they will become eligible to vote, and when they do it will be a one-move checkmate for American liberalism. You are looking at 1.5 to 2 million extra votes going democrat every time. Not only that but tens of thousands of those votes will be in states that consistently lean conservative, such as Texas, Florida, Louisiana and Arizona. If you think Republicans are scarce now, wait ten years. Consider this; if just three thousand illegal aliens had been able to vote in Florida the 2000 election would probably not have been close enough for anything but a cursory recount after which Al Gore would have become President for the last eight years. And right now we *would* be registering our Qu'rans and Bibles with the state.

Politically speaking it is obvious that George Bush made a mistake invading Iraq, but just as in the case of the Supreme Court that is not the end of the story. It may very well be that President Bush felt he was completing the legacy of his father's administration; it does not matter. Today, we have a great open door set before us, and we must take advantage of it if our faiths are to survive. The Muslims are completely right about the way Christian and Jewish believers hide their heads in the sand and proclaim God's promises of protection as an excuse not to get involved. Even as we speak, Haliburton has a government contract to run detention centers for the U.S. government. The press original release is available in the database of KBR archives found online at http://www.haliburton.com/default/main/haliburt on/eng/news/source_files/news.jsp?/newsurl=/def ault/main/haliburton/eng/news/source_files/press _release/2006/kbrmws_012406.html.

For such "ostrich" believers the Book of Esther should be a wake-up call. Just as Mordecai warned Esther, God may very well save the situation through someone else, but the only way you and your family will be saved is if you *personally* act. The same thing happened in the case of the Jews under Hitler; many of those willing to undertake the effort to survive did, and those that did not died. "Never again" must not mean appealing to the United Nations court system, it must mean that we are prepared to defend ourselves from our enemies.

If we are to be prepared to defeat our common enemies, we are going to have to start thinking in radically different terms than we do now. The first and foremost one requires a change in the thinking of the American Church. We need to recognize the ongoing culture war as the central battlefield of our enemy. And we need to understand the dangerous precedent occurring in the American economy.

Slowly but surely the American economic system is being directed back to the Fascist blueprint used in Western Europe and America during World War II. Environmentalism has had a huge impact on the way businesses operate, and those changes set a dangerous course of making American businesses subservient to the State, just as Hitler proclaimed businesses should be. The problem is, if business and government combine forces, governmental power will become an unstoppable force in the U.S. system.

Furthermore, the Church needs to face the hard reality that our unwavering loyalty to America cannot continue as it has. We must remind ourselves that our first loyalty is to God, and that all other loyalties are much less important. The Church through the centuries has prospered under a multitude of different governments, from monarchies to democracies. It is the character of the government that matters most, not the form.

I am not advocating a dictatorship. Certainly American principles are worth supporting, but not always the practices. We like to speak about the idea of loving the sinner but hating the sin and now it is time to apply that principle to our nation.

But wholesale changes to our thinking need to be made across the board by all three faiths. Israelis need to quit pretending that they have the right to run roughshod over their neighbors, and the American Churches must quit supporting their efforts to do so. Israel can no longer afford to pretend the other people in the region are just going to go away. That is their home just as it is yours, and it reflects on your character as well that you cannot find a way to live in peace with them.

And the other peoples of the region need to quit trying to drive the Jews out and worry about working out a deal that will allow them both to share the land in the region. For example, I do not think Israel should necessarily split Jerusalem, but that does not mean they cannot allow the Palestinians to have their capital there as well. Why not put the two governments on neighboring blocks in Jerusalem to make it clear that they cannot continue the current conflict and to represent the fact that their futures are bound to one another whether they like it or not?

Let's assume that tonight the Palestinians conquered the entire region and drove the Israelis out. It might seem like a great victory, but it would not be, because it would be portrayed in the Western media as proof of just how bloodthirsty and irreconcilable Islam is with Western society. It would just be another piece of propaganda leading to American nuclear bombs raining down on Muslim cities. The last thing we need is to provide more fodder to our enemies.

Remember this, my Muslim friends; what the humanists did to the Jews under Hitler they are planning to do to you and me and our families in a single sunny afternoon. You need to settle it in your heart right now that **they will kill us**.

If we are to defend ourselves, what we need is coordinated action, an uprising if you will, that would allow us to limit the power of humanists to assault our values the way they do. And the answer to our dilemma is right there at our hand. We have all of the pieces but for our bull-headedness have not put them together into a single winning strategy.

Most important of all, we must establish a working and united relationship. Right now, all Muslims get to see is American liberals—liberals fornicating on their televisions and handing out condoms in storefront wannabe abortion clinics in India. They do not see that the Church has the same issues they have, because we are not in Iraq helping the people and presenting our case. It is time for Muslims and Christians and Jews to seek one another out.

Where do we start? We start by creating a bank in Dubai or somewhere that is accessible to both Muslims and Christians and Jews and controlled jointly by us. That way we can send resources to wherever they are needed, and we can keep the finances of the bank beyond the reach of the American government. And we can make sure that it follows the principles of our religion concerning usury.

Next, we need to admit and commit to the truth. Here, I am not talking about religious truth per se, but rather what we know about how that truth plays out in everyday life. We know a lot, and we are going to use those truths to our advantage to strengthen ourselves and our peoples.

The first truth we must admit is economic; capitalism is our friend. We are doomed if we do not adopt this position wholeheartedly. The conservative principles that dominated America's economy recently created growth that was staggering, almost beyond imagination, and we need the force of those principles to build up for the future.

Right now, the governments of the Middle East are awash in oil money, but it will not last. Brazil has already found its way to being independent of foreign oil, and the rest of the West will follow soon. Liberals were right about one thing; when gasoline reached about $4 per gallon in the U.S. new technology would prove to be worth exploring as a consequence of the change in relative costs between economies.

This means that ideas like hydrogen vehicles are worth pursuing, because the closer the price of a gasoline vehicle and the fuel it uses over its lifetime comes to the price of the new technology, the more attractive and eventually viable the new technology becomes, and hydrogen may provide a real alternative to oil someday soon. If the transition from oil is carried out effectively, it may well spell the end of oil exports to the West. We need to prepare to move the economies of the Middle East away from oil while they still have economies at all.

And the Churches in America need the economic firepower necessary to withstand the American political system and provide for the acquisition of weapons. Whether we like it or not the American government is going to come for us sometime within the decade or so, and we will suffer the fate of the Jews under Hitler if we do not prepare to fight back.

In Lebanon, Hezbollah runs many businesses, providing income for the organization and jobs in an area where they are desperately needed. I would like to see that process continued and expanded to other areas of the Middle East and America through trust funds that provide access to capital and funds for our religious organizations. It is unacceptable that after all the years American troops have been in Iraq, the Iraqis have to try to beg Iran to build them electrical plants. That must be our first project.

The only caveat is that free enterprise must come first. Economically speaking, Hezbollah and other groups that run businesses must be treated just like any other business in the area. That way those groups can avoid the appearance of gangsterism while allowing the economy there to expand more than they could grow it alone. Muslims and Christians alike must accept the conservative principles of economics put forth in the last few decades and proven to work. We must abandon the sick ideas of the disease of socialism, and I call on Bin Laden to renounce socialist ideals.

The second truth we need to admit is the nature of government, particularly what it can and cannot do. According to nationmaster.com the United States ranks 24th in murders per 100,000 people. But it is also true that not a single Islamic country ranks above the United States in this statistic.

The liberal reply to this is that the difference comes from the nature of Islamic and American cultures. I disagree, because there have been times in American history when nationally or regionally we have approached similar murder rates to Islamic countries, and as the culture in America changed the murder rate changed with it.

The question then is what part the American government should play in the process of cultural change. The liberal view is that government should be the central tool of social change. I contend that the government has the responsibility to follow the dictions of society as it does in certain Islamic countries such as Saudi Arabia.

Here liberals offer up the argument that while it is acceptable to use government to reorganize society and promote immorality, "you can't legislate morality". I believe the opposite is true; government can *only* legislate morality and protect individuals from being harmed by the economic and personal activities of others, just as is written in our scriptures.

Legislating morality is, in fact, precisely what government does, and one of the few things it does well. When the state creates a law that punishes murder, it agrees with scripture that murder is morally wrong. And the extraordinary drop in crime that occurred in New York under Rudy Guiliani is further evidence that when "good" is enforced across the board in any given area, the cultural temperament of that area changes and crimes become less common.

So what we need, both in Muslim countries and in America, are governments that operate based on these ideas of universal morality. In Islamic countries this is easy enough but not in America. What we need in America is a way of resetting things and getting rid of most of the monstrosity that has become the federal government, which is more interested in keeping people from smoking than in fighting crime. Whether we like it or not, it just might be time to overthrow the current American government.

Fortunately there is a tool which just might help us do exactly that. In America we have something called a homeowner's association, in which the people who live in a closed neighborhood or set of condos agree to live by a particular set of rules and usually receive some sort of property management. In return the association has the right to tell people they have to keep their grass mowed and the hedges trimmed.

So what if people had a Christian homeowner's association where they agreed not to steal and that blocked the Playboy channel? What we need is for the Churches to create a homeowner's association that could do this for both businesses and homeowners, buying back the homes and businesses of people who did not live up to community standards and forcing them to leave the community.

But I do not suggest creating a giant monastery; these communities need to be open, where anyone can live if they will keep the rules. The idea is to show people that these economic and moral ideas work in the long haul. I believe that such communities would prove far more successful than the "normal" communities nearby.

Here is the sticking point; this plan will not go unchallenged by the government, either locally or federally. So those in the community must agree to defend it from the government at large. Waco was such a black eye to the Clinton administration because the federal agents had little provocation to respond as they did. In fact, it was similar circumstances that led to the founding of America. Public opinion turned against the British because the people saw the government abuse its power.

To this end we need to make sure that our communities are not in the middle of some stretch of unused prairie. We want people to see the successful expansion of our communities and how the government responds. The American public might not care if the federal government knocks down some house built on the side of a mountain somewhere but Americans will respond differently when it happens next to the off ramp to their own houses. Let the government come to us, and we will have a revolution with public support, fought against a government that has become what the British government used to be to the colonists; belligerent, overbearing and controlled by special interests.

The goal is not just to reset the culture and tip the tide back in our direction, but to make permanent changes in the framework of our society. Frankly, we need to change the constitution. Not wholesale changes, just a few tweaks here and there.

For example, we need a marriage amendment defining a marriage as between a man and a woman. We need to get rid of the establishment of religion provision in the Bill of Rights and replace it with the statement "The right to religious expression may not be hampered, either publicly or privately". And we need to fix the number of Supreme Court Justices at nine, three of which are to be appointed by the Churches, Mosques, and Synagogues of America.

Furthermore, we need to get rid of the free speech amendment, replacing it with the right to all *political* speech instead. That way we could stem the flow of filth being poured into our homes through the American media without unduly limiting the ability to redress government and protest government action or discuss public policy. Christians have proven to be excellent at media production, and our greatest successes recently have come through our media productions. We will not run short of programming without pornography—barring another writer strike someday.

And while we are at it we could get rid of the Department of Education and the National Endowment for the Arts. During the Reagan Revolution, the conservatives failed to uproot government institutions that provided liberals cover to disseminate their poison and keep their failing ideas alive in American society. I suggest we not make that mistake again.

So what can we do right now? We can begin with that bank I was talking about. We can start pressuring our ministers to come together and begin creating those homeowner's associations. We can begin to organize trust funds to oversee our operations, and allow them to be bequeathed to our faith organizations with out own management teams.

And we can start putting enough money into our new bank to build that power plant in Baghdad so the economy there can expand and we can invest even more in Iraq. And we could put our money together and use our new bank to buy Adelphia Communications so we could start stemming the flow of filth pouring out of American companies.

Eventually we could put our own satellite up in the Middle East which will show programming that we can approve of as people of faith. We can then deliver a warning to the people who own the satellites that deliver media garbage to the Muslim people; turn it off or we shoot it down. We can, if we choose to, stand together against those who would destroy us. That is the one outcome of the Iraq War which would undo the programme of American liberals.

It is possible to change things, but we are going to have to think outside the box like

Hezbollah did when it started running businesses in Lebanon. One thing is clear; we cannot just sit back and allow our faiths be destroyed by the new liberal culture war. These are our beliefs, and they are universal goods that even people who never set foot in a Church or Mosque or Synagogue live better lives by following and living by.

What we need are not just people willing to die for the cause, but a strategy that allows us to show the world they should live for it, that our beliefs create benefits that cannot be gotten through humanism and its evil stepchildren. If we do this, we will win. If we do not, all is lost. There is one thing I believe the Bible makes clear in both the New and Old Testaments; it is not our successes but our failures that lead to the end of days.

www.ingramcontent.com/pod-product-compliance
Lightning Source LLC
Chambersburg PA
CBHW030415100426
42812CB00028B/2975/J